Children with Down's Syndrome

A Guide for Teachers and Learning Support
Assistants in Mainstream Primary
and Secondary Schools

Stephanie Lorenz

David Fulton Publishers
London

David Fulton Publishers Ltd
Ormond House, 26–27 Boswell Street, London WC1N 3JZ

www.fultonpublishers.co.uk

First published in Great Britain by David Fulton Publishers 1998
Reprinted 1999, 2000, 2001

Note: The right of Stephanie Lorenz to be identified as the author of this work has been asserted by her in accordance with the Copyright, Designs and Patents Act 1988.

British Library Cataloguing in Publication Data
A catalogue record for this book is available from the British Library

ISBN 1–85346–506–2

Typeset by Textype Typesetters, Cambridge
Printed in Great Britain by Bell and Bain Ltd, Glasgow

Contents

Acknowledgements

Thanks are due firstly to Janice Pickering, David and Pat Storey, James and Elaine Nicol, David Barnes and Carolyn Loveday, Jeanette Aumeed, Ann Warrington, Julie Shuker, Carole Leedham, Fran Russell, Lorraine Brown, Sylvia Alty, Rochelle Abrahams, Trish Spendiffe, Nicola Pearcey and all the other parents whose commitment to inclusive education inspired me to write this book.

To Paul Sibbons, June Wilson and all the staff at John Smeaton High School, who convinced me that inclusion at secondary level could be a reality, I extend particular thanks. The materials and data they provided have been invaluable. Mark Vaughan at the Centre for Studies on Inclusive Education (CSIE) kindly allowed me to use their '10 Reasons for Inclusion', while Julie Wong let me read and take extracts from the delightful letters she received when seeking a secondary school place for her daughter Chantal. Jane Beadman of the Devon Psychological Service gave me access to her excellent training materials and her recent evaluation of the placement of children with Down's Syndrome in South Devon. Her generosity is greatly appreciated.

Bob Black and Eric Nicholas of the Down's Syndrome Association (DSA) have provided unfailing encouragement and support throughout the project and have cheered me up when the enormity of the task started to get me down. Particular thanks are due to Eric, who read every word of my first draft and translated it into English, and to the friends and colleagues who took the time to read the final version and offer helpful suggestions. I would especially like to thank Joyce Berry, Margaret Graham, Phyllis Ward, Moira Greensmith and Liz Myall.

Finally, my thanks must go to my husband Roger for his forbearance and meticulous proofreading. Any mistakes are entirely his fault.

This book is dedicated to Ross, Sukainah, Andrew, David, Selina, Mark, Timothy, Lucy, Jamie, Ailsa and all the other children with Down's Syndrome it has been my pleasure to know.

Chapter 1
What is Down's Syndrome?

Introduction

What we now know as Down's Syndrome was first described, in 1866, by John Langdon Down, a physician at the Earlswood Asylum for Idiots, in England. He attempted to classify the inmates into separate ethnic groups, using characteristics such as hair type, bone structure and skin colour. He proposed that the feeble-minded should be classified into racial types such as Ethiopian, Aztec, Malay or Mongolian.

While the other categories rapidly fell into disuse, the term 'mongol', for those with Down's Syndrome, gained universal acceptance and is still used, in some quarters, to this day. Interestingly enough, although most British parents find the term 'mongol' offensive, some in The Netherlands, fighting for the inclusion of their children in mainstream schools, continue to use the term interchangeably with that of Down's Syndrome. For, as they say: 'Neither of the two terms is in fact appropriate. The problem remains that both labels continue to locate the problem exclusively in the child itself. Basically, however, there is no medical problem, but a social one' (De Wit 1994).

Causes of Down's Syndrome

Down's Syndrome is a genetic condition, caused by a failure in the cell division process. The majority of affected children have a third copy of chromosome 21 in all their cells, instead of the usual two, and this results in the baby having 47 chromosomes instead of 46. In medical literature, Down's Syndrome is often referred to as trisomy 21 for this reason. While the condition has been recognised since the middle of the 19th century, its genetic basis was not discovered until 1959, when Professor Jerome Lejeune, in Paris, first identified the characteristic combination of chromosomes.

In normal development, the baby grows, by cell division, from an embryo produced by the fusion of an egg and a sperm. Each of these sex cells normally contains 23 individual chromosomes, representing one half of those found in all other types of body cell. In the formation of the sex cells, each pair of chromosomes divides, providing the genetic material for two eggs or two sperm. However, occasionally, the two versions of chromosome 21 fail to separate and move together into the same sex cell.

The abnormal sex cells, thus formed, stand the same chance of fertilisation as other unaffected eggs or sperm. An embryo with only 45 chromosomes is most unlikely to survive. However, one with 47 will develop and grow in the normal way, but will produce a baby with Down's Syndrome. While approximately 90 per cent of babies with Down's Syndrome receive their extra chromosome in this way from their mother (see Figure 1.1), just under 5 per cent receive the extra genetic material from their father. At this point in time, no one is clear what causes faulty cell division, although certain factors, notably maternal age, increase the risk. Any couple, from any social, cultural or racial background, can produce a baby with Down's Syndrome.

The process described above accounts for just over 95 per cent of embryos with Down's Syndrome. Of the remaining 5 per cent of instances, approximately half

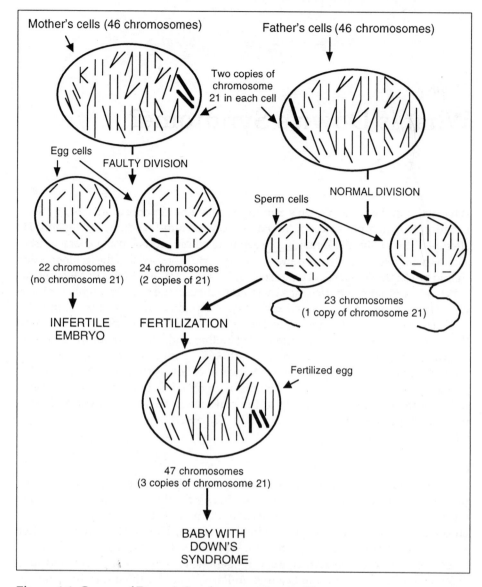

Figure 1.1 Causes of Down's Syndrome – trisomy 21

are due to what is termed a translocation. In these cases, two of one parent's chromosomes are joined together and so do not separate properly when the sex cells are formed. As a result the baby will have the usual two copies of chromosome 21, plus some additional 21st chromosome material. Affected parents, while showing none of the signs of Down's Syndrome, will be carriers and so are at risk of producing more than one child with the syndrome. They may also pass on the translocation to their normally developing children, who will also be carriers. In such cases, genetic counselling is generally recommended.

In the remaining instances, the baby is born with a mosaic form of Down's Syndrome. Here, the embryo is produced from two normal sex cells, but then develops a trisomy as the cells continue to divide. Where a fault develops at a very early stage in division, a significant proportion of the baby's cells will contain the extra chromosome. As a consequence, the effects will be no different from those found in other forms of Down's Syndrome. Where cell division goes wrong at a much later stage, the effects may be reduced or even negligible. However, each case will be unique. Certainly there is no evidence to suggest that the majority of children with mosaic Down's Syndrome are significantly different from those with full trisomy 21.

On average in the UK, two babies are born every day with Down's Syndrome. One in 1,000 new-born babies will be affected, approximately 700 in any one year. Although the risk of producing a baby with Down's Syndrome increases from around 1 in 2,000 at the age of 20, to 1 in 18 at the age of 45, most babies with Down's Syndrome have always been born to younger mothers, since the overall birth rate is higher in this age group.

Unlike many other forms of developmental disorder, Down's Syndrome can now be diagnosed at birth, or even in the womb, by means of a straightforward chromosome analysis. In many areas of the country, all mothers are now offered a blood test, such as the triple test, in the early stages of pregnancy. This screening procedure aims to identify those with high levels of three substances known to correlate with the incidence of Down's Syndrome. The results are entered into a computer program, which also takes account of maternal age and other relevant family factors, and a level of risk is generated. On the basis of this result, parents are offered the opportunity to have an amniocentesis, which samples cells from the amniotic fluid around the baby, or chorionic villus sampling (CVS), which takes cells directly from the placenta.

Screening procedures are improving all the time. Nevertheless, their reliability is still quite low. Many mothers with a high risk go on to produce a normal baby, while others, with a low risk, give birth to a baby with Down's Syndrome. The diagnostic tests, on the other hand, despite increasing the probability of miscarriage, will establish with a high degree of certainty whether the baby is affected by Down's Syndrome since they actually count the chromosomes.

Once a positive result has been given, the family have then to decide whether they wish the pregnancy to be terminated. Although the increasing availability of prenatal screening and abortion of affected embryos has substantially reduced the number of older mothers giving birth to babies with Down's Syndrome, many parents are reluctant to take the tests because of the high level of stress generated and the increased risk to the baby. Others, opposed to abortion, are happy to accept their baby as it is and reject the whole screening concept on ethical grounds.

Physical development

Babies with Down's Syndrome can generally be recognised at birth by their distinctive facial features, as well as by other physical signs (Figure 1.2). However, there appears to be no relationship between the obviousness of these physical characteristics and the degree to which their development is delayed. Many of the features considered to be typical of Down's Syndrome are due to incomplete growth of the skull and skeletal system – e.g. some bones remain underdeveloped, giving rise to the typical short stature, slanting eyes and flat face.

Small sinuses, narrow canals in the middle ear and an increased risk of respiratory infection, lead to a higher-than-average incidence of conductive hearing loss. Hearing difficulties are generally treated by draining off excess fluid and inserting grommets or, increasingly, by the fitting of hearing aids. This latter course is often favoured for even mild hearing losses, as grommets frequently fail to fit the small ear canals of young children with Down's Syndrome and tend to get gummed up by characteristically viscous mucus. While over 50 per cent of children with Down's Syndrome are likely to suffer from a conductive hearing loss, due to glue ear, up to 20 per cent may, instead, have a sensorineural loss, caused by developmental defects in the inner ear or the auditory nerves.

Visual problems are even more prevalent, and around 60–70 per cent of young children with Down's Syndrome are prescribed spectacles before the age of seven. Some 40 per cent of children with Down's Syndrome show a degree of

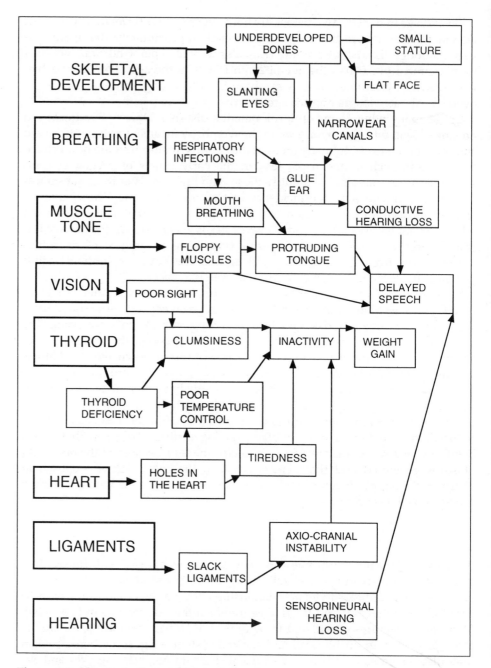

Figure 1.2 Physical effects of Down's Syndrome

long-sightedness, while up to 14 per cent may be short-sighted. Astigmatism, squints and lens disorders also occur more frequently than in the population as a whole. However, all these conditions can be treated effectively.

Poor muscle tone is very common in babies with Down's Syndrome and leads to delayed motor milestones and a tendency to clumsiness. These can, in turn, act as a discouragement to the child beginning to explore the environment and lead to inactivity and consequently to overweight. Similar effects can, however, result from an underactive thyroid – a condition found in at least 15 per cent of people with Down's Syndrome. Where there is any doubt about thyroid functioning, routine blood tests are recommended.

An underactive thyroid can also affect the ability of the young child to regulate body temperature. Similarly, a child with a heart condition may get chilled in extreme weather conditions, turning blue around the lips or fingers. Congenital heart disorders are found in up to 50 per cent of children with Down's Syndrome. In many cases, slight murmurs require no medical intervention and pose no significant health risk. In others, corrective surgery is imperative. However, most operations are now successful and the children concerned can go on to lead full and active lives.

Weak muscles in the tongue and mouth, combined with obstructed nasal passages, lead many young children with Down's Syndrome to become mouth breathers and to protrude their tongues. While relatively small jaw bones in some children with Down's Syndrome make the tongue seem rather larger than in other children, tongue-lolling can be effectively controlled by exercise and encouragement. Certainly, few people in the field would recommend that parents recourse to plastic surgery to reduce tongue size.

A great source of anxiety to some parents and teachers is the risk of neck fracture or dislocation. Many children are prevented from doing forward rolls or using the trampoline because of these concerns. While we know that slack neck ligaments, combined with poorly formed vertebrae, increase the risk of neck dislocation in some children with Down's Syndrome, this atlanto-axial instability is rare. In most cases, it is not considered necessary to prevent young people with Down's Syndrome from taking part in the full range of physical activities. Nevertheless, parents and teachers need to be aware of the symptoms and problems that can arise from sporting or whiplash injuries. To allay any anxieties, a useful leaflet on the subject can be obtained from the Down's Syndrome Association.

Learning and behaviour

All children with Down's Syndrome show some delay in their development, although they vary widely in their learning ability. While each is a unique individual, with his or her own combination of strengths and weaknesses, some common threads in development can be identified. Work by Faulkener and Lewis (1995), suggests that development in young people with Down's Syndrome is different from that of normally developing children and not merely delayed. Studies by a range of authors (e.g. Bower and Hayes, 1994), have found particular delays in the development of short-term auditory memory skills. These were found to be significantly greater than in other children of equivalent intellectual ability, although their performance on visual memory tasks was roughly the same.

There is also evidence that children with Down's Syndrome make poor use of skills that have been acquired. Wishart (1993) concludes that they are less well motivated than other learners of a similar developmental level and tend to adopt behavioural strategies that undermine the progress of their learning. Teachers may find that social behaviours, such as playing the fool, are used by the child to distract adult attention and so avoid tasks seen as too difficult, too easy or too much trouble. The characteristic 'stubbornness' of many children with Down's Syndrome may reflect this tendency.

On starting school at age five, the most able children with Down's Syndrome are often functioning near an average level for their age. At the other end of the ability range, children with Down's Syndrome can be found who have severe difficulties or additional problems due to unrelated conditions such as autism, Attention Deficit Disorder (ADD) or epilepsy. Lorenz (1984), tested 115 children on the Stanford-Binet Intelligence Scale at five to seven years of age and found an IQ range from 10 to 92, with the girls achieving a mean of 48 and the boys a mean of 42 (see Figure 1.3). While children with Down's Syndrome were considered ineducable until 1970, it would now appear that a significant proportion of children with the syndrome (36 per cent in the author's sample), have only mild or moderate learning difficulties. It is also clear that their skills continue to develop throughout life.

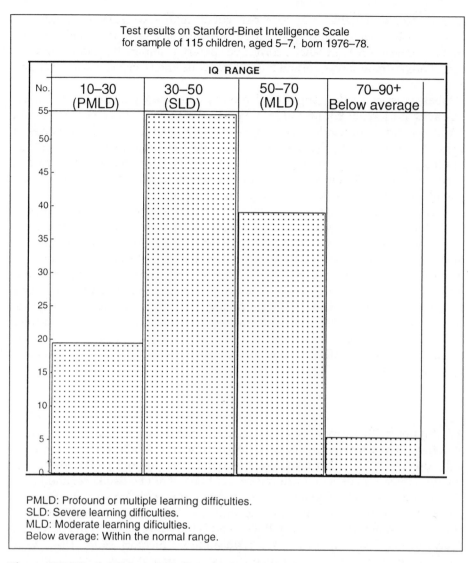

Test results on Stanford-Binet Intelligence Scale
for sample of 115 children, aged 5–7, born 1976–78.

PMLD: Profound or multiple learning difficulties.
SLD: Severe learning difficulties.
MLD: Moderate learning dificulties.
Below average: Within the normal range.

Figure 1.3 IQ of children with Down's Syndrome

Although there is no doubt that the measured IQ of children with Down's Syndrome does decline with age, rates of progress vary greatly and no evidence exists to support the widely held view that the overall development of children with Down's Syndrome reaches a plateau in adolescence. Certainly, care needs to be taken in the use of psychometric instruments with this population. Work by Wishart (1996) indicates that the performance of children with Down's Syndrome can fluctuate greatly over identical, closely spaced testing sessions. Rather than practice improving performance, as might be expected, she found that some items, completed successfully on the first trial, were subsequently failed.

Even when similar scores were obtained by children with Down's Syndrome and others who were developing normally, she found that the two groups responded quite differently in the test situation. Since it is now becomingly increasingly clear that the developmental progress of children with Down's Syndrome is actually quite different from that of their normally developing peers, conclusions drawn from tests standardised on the normal population must be interpreted with considerable caution.

Chapter 2
Inclusive Education

In April 1971, all children with Down's Syndrome were given the right to education for the first time. Prior to this, the 1899 Elementary Education (Defective and Epileptic Children) Act remained in force. Under this Act, children who were considered incapable of receiving instruction in ordinary schools were divided into those who would benefit from placement in special classes or schools and those who were considered ineducable. The vast majority of children with Down's Syndrome were placed in this latter category.

The Mental Deficiency Act (1913) formalised the process of categorising children by requiring Local Education Authorities (LEAs) to ascertain and certify which children aged 7 to 16 in their area were defective. This duty was carried out by medical officers, who administered standardised intelligence tests. Those children who failed to achieve an IQ of 50 were passed to the care of the local mental deficiency committee. Some of these children remained at home and attended a health authority-run Training Centre. Others ended up in long-stay subnormality hospitals where they remained for the rest of their lives.

As Mason and Rieser (1994) note, the 1970 (Handicapped Children) Act gave some 70,000 ineducable children the label Educationally Subnormal (Severe) and the right to their own brand of special education. Approximately 400 new special schools were created in England and Wales for this population of children, most of them from existing Junior Training Centres. While qualified teachers, many specially trained to work with the mentally handicapped, were gradually added to the care staff already in post, practices changed very little for many years. Medical officers continued to play a key role in the assessment of children with learning difficulties, although there was a gradual transfer of responsibility from the doctor to the educational psychologist. However, standardised measures of intelligence remained the principal means by which children were categorised.

In 1978, the Warnock Committee of Enquiry into children with special educational needs published its findings. It rejected the previously held view that there existed a clear distinction between handicapped and ordinary children. Instead, it talked about a continuum of special educational need which had to be met by a continuum of provision. Although the report never suggested that all disabled children should be placed in mainstream settings, it certainly gave a boost to the notion of integration, taking on board the American concept of least restrictive environment enshrined in the Federal Education for All Handicapped Children Act (1974). Expressing a personal view, Mary Warnock (1982) clearly stated her hope and belief that 'there will not be many Down's Syndrome children left in special schools in a few years time'.

By the early 1980s, a few LEAs were already supporting the integration of young people with a learning disability into mainstream schools, either on an individual basis or in groups to form an attached unit. A number of these initiatives are described by Hegarty and Pocklington (1982). Due to geographical or other factors, some areas of the country had never invested in separate special schools and, as a consequence, had always placed disabled

A history of inclusion

7

children in the mainstream. Others, responding to the Warnock Report, had made an explicit commitment to integration, which resulted in significant changes in practice.

At the same time, many LEAs were recognising that not all students with Down's Syndrome had severe learning difficulties (SLD) and, increasingly, children with Down's Syndrome were being placed in schools or units for pupils with moderate learning difficulties (MLD). Studies by Moorcroft-Cuckle (1993) and Shepperdson (1995) illustrate this trend.

A survey of the placement of children with Down's Syndrome in one northern LEA (Lorenz, 1995) found that prior to 1981, the vast majority were placed in SLD schools. However, the implementation of the 1981 Act resulted first in a move from SLD to MLD provision and subsequently to placements in the mainstream. Of those students reaching the age of five between 1980 and 1983, 70 per cent were placed in SLD schools and virtually none in the mainstream. Of those reaching five between 1984–5, 77 per cent were placed initially in MLD schools, while by 1986–7, 59 per cent of five-year-olds with Down's Syndrome were being placed in their local mainstream primary.

Despite a similar move towards mainstream placements in a few other areas of the country, prejudice continued to be held against students with Down's Syndrome who looked mentally handicapped. For example, Booth and Potts (1983) report that the special unit at one school was apparently referred to as the 'mong wing'.

Inclusion today

The 1981 Education Act and the 1993 Act which consolidated it, encouraged LEAs to integrate students with special needs into the mainstream, in accordance with parental wishes. However, it also provided three let-out clauses for those LEAs that were committed to segregated provision. An LEA only has a duty to integrate a child with special educational needs, in accordance with parental wishes, provided the placement is compatible with:

- the child receiving the special educational provision which his or her learning difficulty calls for,
- the interests of other children in the school, and
- the efficient use of resources.

As digests of recent cases from the Special Educational Needs (SEN) Tribunal have shown, some LEAs are regularly using these clauses to over-ride parental preference and impose segregated provision. Thus in one case, in 1995, the Tribunal accepted the LEA view that were a 12-year-old boy with Down's Syndrome to transfer from a mainstream primary to a grant maintained secondary school 'He would not take part in appropriate learning experiences for most of the time'.

After hearing the LEA's case, they accepted that 'the specialist teaching in the smaller more controlled environment of the special school would be more suitable to his ability, aptitude and special needs'.

Interestingly enough, a subsequent Tribunal overturned the earlier ruling and, according to his parents, the young man is now happily attending a local comprehensive.

In some instances, however, LEA attempts to use the 1993 Act to impose segregation have not been supported by Tribunal panels. In a recent case (Capper, 1997), the Tribunal accepted that a mainstream placement would cost several thousand pounds more than a special school place. Nevertheless, in its conclusion, the panel stated that 'we have to take account of wider issues such as the value obtained from the proposed expenditure'.

In their view 'greater value would be obtained in terms of likely educational

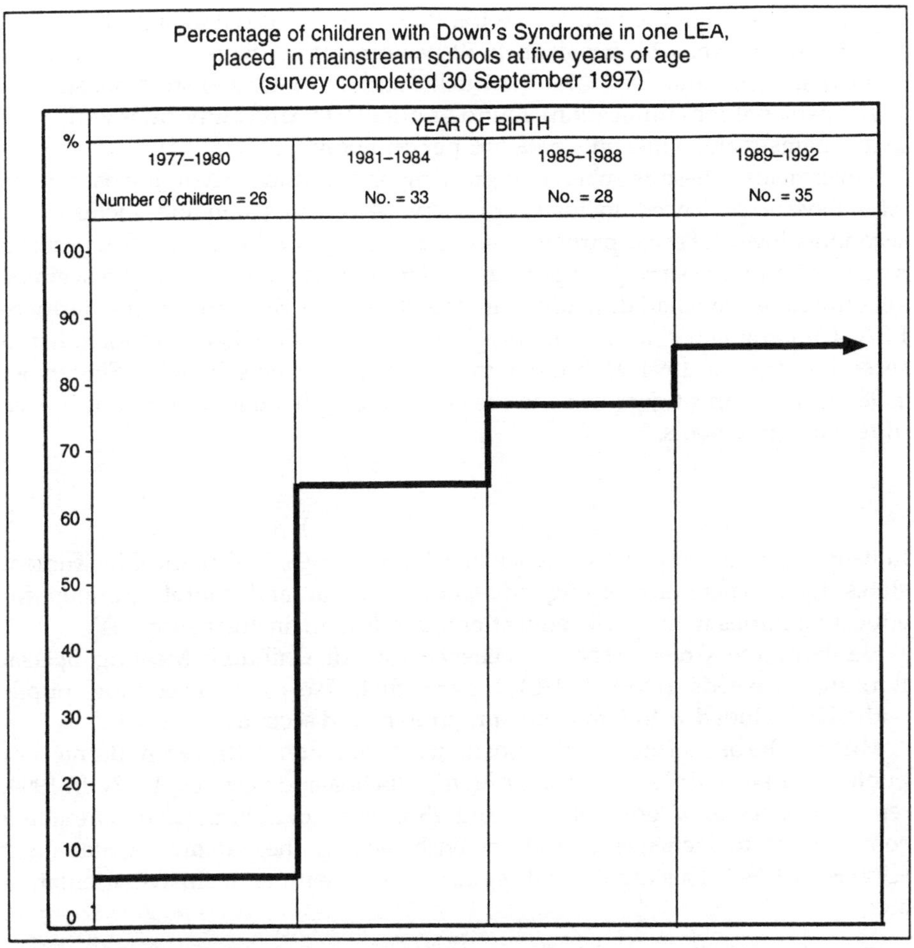

Percentage of children with Down's Syndrome in one LEA,
placed in mainstream schools at five years of age
(survey completed 30 September 1997)

%	YEAR OF BIRTH			
	1977–1980	1981–1984	1985–1988	1989–1992
	Number of children = 26	No. = 33	No. = 28	No. = 35

Figure 2.1 Inclusion of children with Down's Syndrome

progress, stimulation of expressive language and social interaction in the mainstream school'.

Inclusive placement, therefore, would constitute an efficient use of resources. On this occasion, the panel found for the parents, although such a far-sighted interpretation of the law does not appear to be the norm. Progress towards greater inclusion for children with Down's Syndrome continues steadily. Nevertheless, the position nationally is still very patchy. An extension of the author's survey in the same LEA (see Figure 2.1), found that in 1997, 83 per cent of five-year-old pupils with Down's Syndrome were being placed in mainstream schools.

However, a similar survey by Cuckle (1997), who gathered her data via local health authority records, found a rather less optimistic picture. While the most inclusive quarter of the 94 health districts reported 67 per cent or more of their children placed in the mainstream at five to six years of age, there were still 23 districts who had 28 per cent or less. Even today, there is still a small minority of LEAs in which no child with Down's Syndrome has been offered a mainstream place without recourse to Tribunal. Hopefully, this should not be the case for much longer, as parents use their new powers to secure the schools of their choice.

Although in most LEAs a high proportion of parents who request a mainstream place for a primary-aged child with Down's Syndrome is now successful, the position for students at secondary level is considerably less encouraging. Even in those LEAs most committed to inclusive education, substantially fewer students with Down's Syndrome are placed in mainstream high schools than in the primary sector. Booth (1996) looked at eight LEAs and found a range from 2.5 per cent to 50 per cent of students aged 11 to 16 in mainstream secondary schools. The Cuckle survey, looking at students aged 14 to 16, (personal communication), found 42 out of 94 health authorities with none in the mainstream, while only 5 had 50 per cent or more.

Nevertheless, these numbers are growing and attitudes changing as parents who have experienced inclusive primary placements demand inclusion at secondary level. Of those parents of secondary aged children, who took part in a recent nation-wide survey, 30 per cent had to fight to gain a primary placement yet only 26 per cent had difficulties at secondary level. Similarly, in one northern LEA (Cunningham *et al.* 1997), only 25 per cent of students were included at secondary level in 1994, all but one in a single resourced school. By September 1998, however, this figure had increased to 70%, with students attending seven different high schools.

Reasons for inclusion

In its recent White Paper 'Excellence in Schools' (DfEE, 1997a), the Government states that: 'There are strong educational, social and moral grounds for educating pupils with special educational needs in mainstream schools'.

Similarly, the Green Paper 'Excellence for All Children: Meeting Special Educational Needs' (DfEE 1997b) declares that: 'We want to see more pupils with SEN included within mainstream primary and secondary schools.'

Much of the background to this position can be found in the recent Barnardo's publication *What works in inclusive education* (Sebba and Sachdev, 1997). In 1994, representatives of 92 governments and 25 international organisations made a commitment to inclusive education, enshrined in the Salamanca Statement (UNESCO 1994). This argues that regular schools with an inclusive orientation are:

> The most effective means of combating discriminatory attitudes, creating welcoming communities, building an inclusive society and achieving education for all; moreover they provide an effective education to the majority of children and improve the efficiency and ultimately the cost-effectiveness of the entire education system.

Legislation to support the move towards inclusion has existed in the USA since 1975, in Italy since 1977 (Newbold, 1997) and in Canada since 1982. Sweden and Denmark have also moved a long way towards a more inclusive system (Glaesel, 1997). Practice elsewhere in Europe, however, has tended to be more traditional, with an emphasis on special schools or classes. Although some children with Down's Syndrome are now being integrated into schools in Spain (Lopez, 1994) and in the Netherlands (Scheepstra *et al.*, 1996), they still operate largely segregated systems, as do other European countries such as Germany and Belgium (Meijer *et al.*, 1994).

The Campaign for Studies on Inclusive Education (CSIE, 1996) outlines ten reasons for inclusion (see Figure 2.2).

While there are few who would argue with the human rights position or the aim of working towards a more tolerant society, there are many educationalists and parents who are still to be convinced that mainstream placement will provide the best possible educational and social experience for all children with Down's Syndrome. Some professionals still hold the view that only the most able pupils with Down's Syndrome are able to benefit from inclusive education. Thus in many LEAs mainstream placements are offered only to those young people who obtain a predetermined score on an intelligence test, have achieved at a particular level in National Curriculum assessments, or are able to perform at an agreed level on a standardised test of reading or number. In other areas of

TEN REASONS FOR INCLUSION

Inclusive education is a human right, it's good education and it makes good social sense.

HUMAN RIGHTS

1. All children have the right to learn together.

2. Children should not be devalued or discriminated against by being excluded or sent away because of their disability or learning difficulty.

3. Disabled adults, describing themselves as special school survivors, are demanding an end to segregation.

4. There are no legitimate reasons to separate children for their education. Children belong together – with advantages and benefits for everyone. They do not need to be protected from each other.

GOOD EDUCATION

5. Research shows children do better academically and socially in integrated settings.

6. There is no teaching or care in a segregated school which cannot take place in an ordinary school.

7. Given commitment and support, inclusive education is a more efficient use of educational resources.

GOOD SOCIAL SENSE

8. Segregation teaches children to be fearful, ignorant and breeds prejudice.

9. All children need an education that will help them develop relationships and prepare them for life in the mainstream.

10. Only inclusion has the potential to reduce fear and to build friendship, respect and understanding.

Figure 2.2

the country, selection is based on levels of language development, self-help skill or behaviour.

Most of the evidence upon which these crucial decisions are based, is gathered on a one-to-one-basis, or in a setting quite different from that in which the parent is seeking placement. Experience suggests that this type of evidence is at best unreliable as a predictor of successful inclusion and at worst totally misleading. Not only is the test performance of children with Down's Syndrome erratic, but also their profile of skills renders many of the most commonly used instruments inappropriate. Despite good visual perceptual skills, the preschool child with Down's Syndrome may well fail practical matching or sorting tasks because of clumsy finger movements. Poor auditory memory and a longer than average response time are likely to reduce the quality of performance on items that rely on verbal instructions or are timed, despite the child's ability to understand the task and complete it satisfactorily under different conditions.

Many children with poor levels of skill at a preschool level are encouraged by the example of more able peers to extend their repertoire or consolidate emergent skills through practice. Parents who have battled with toilet training at home, may find their young children following friends to the toilet once they start school. Extensive work by Sue Buckley and her colleagues in Portsmouth (e.g. Buckley and Bird, 1993) has demonstrated convincingly that children with little or no expressive language can learn to read accurately and with understanding. Rather than being a prerequisite, expressive language develops alongside the child's reading.

At the secondary stage, parents and schools have found that National Curriculum Levels of 2 or below need not be a bar to successful inclusion. Many secondary schools nowadays, have experience of catering for pupils with a wide range of special needs, some entering high school as non-readers or unable to produce written work without access to technological aids. Where schools are willing to look flexibly at their curriculum and use support creatively, many young people with Down's Syndrome are benefiting greatly from mainstream placement. As one parent commented (Lincoln *et al.*, 1992), her 13 year-old-son 'has returned home uttering French phrases, clutching delights such as rhubarb crumble (intact), an electrical circuit which lights up a funny face and homework he has tackled unaided – achievements we thought would never be possible'.

Rather than looking towards assessment of the child alone in determining the appropriateness of inclusion, available evidence suggests that of far greater significance are the attitudes of the other people involved. Petley (1994) in her study of ten children with Down's Syndrome placed in mainstream schools concluded that the attitude of the school was crucial. Experience suggests that if schools are positive about the placement, they will deal with the inevitable hiccups using a practical problem-solving approach. Comments from one middle school, writing in response to a parental enquiry about the school's experiences in including a child with Down's Syndrome, illustrate this point very well:

> There have been problems . . . but it has all been worthwhile. Simon is independent, confident, popular, happy and has a wicked sense of humour. We will all be really upset when he leaves next summer – not a soul will breathe a sigh of relief because he has never been a burden or an unwanted problem. He has been a delight to teach.

Where schools are apprehensive and fearful, difficulties will be perceived as evidence of an inappropriate placement and little will be done to address the problem directly. Instead, pressure is likely to be placed on the parents to visit special schools and consider segregated provision. Preparation of the school, before the child starts and support for staff throughout the child's education are therefore key features in ensuring a successful placement. With advice and training from the LEA, as well as an appropriate level of resourcing, there is no reason why a place in a local school should not be offered to every child with Down's Syndrome, at least in the early years. Despite this, some parents will still opt for a more specialised and protected placement. However, it is they, rather than the LEA, who should be making that decision.

Nevertheless, in some areas of the country, LEAs are still reluctant to go the whole way and instead favour mixed placements. In these instances, the child attends a mainstream school on a part-time basis, while remaining on the roll of the special school. Such provision is said to give the child the best of both worlds. In reality it presents him or her with additional difficulties. For a child who is slow to learn rules, a shared placement can create real confusion, particularly if the expectations of the two settings are quite different. As a consequence, the child may become unsettled and present management problems. Children given a trial placement in mainstream on a part-time basis, may be unable to adjust and are then, unfairly, deemed to be unsuited to inclusive provision.

Alternative models

Friendships often fail to develop where children with Down's Syndrome are only in the school part-time. They are seen as visitors by their peers and so are not included in party invitation lists intended to include the whole class. Schnorr (1990) reported that a seven-year-old with Down's Syndrome, attending part-time, was not regarded as a true member of the class even though he had his own desk. Socially children did not engage in play with him, nor was he identified as a friend by any of his classmates. This experience is very different from that of children fully included in mainstream classes. Allen (1987) writing about one child's experience of inclusive education described her as enjoying 'a full social life amongst the children who live on her modern, private, housing estate'.

Part-timers may not be involved in school events such as the Christmas concert if their pattern of attendance means that they are not available for rehearsals. Responsibility for their educational programme tends to remain with the special school. Often, part-time children have no mainstream Individual Education Plan (IEP) and are perceived as attending purely for social reasons. Thus opportunities to benefit from a more challenging curriculum and good models of learning are frequently missed.

If mixed placements are to be successful, it is essential that mainstream and special school staff plan together on a regular basis. Because of time constraints, this is rarely possible unless the mainstream school chosen is close to the special school. As a consequence, children with Down's Syndrome may be offered a place in a mainstream school a long way from home. While convenient from the point of view of transport and planning, such placements deny the child the chance to make friends with children from their own community. This is particularly significant in the early years when friendships are being established.

Another approach to inclusion, favoured by some LEAs, is to create resourced primary schools to which children with additional needs are directed. Such placements are often seen, by LEAs, as the most cost-effective way of distributing scarce resources. Nevertheless, they too present major problems for the child with Down's Syndrome. In offering the child access to a mainstream curriculum and a normally developing peer group, within a resourced school, many LEAs believe that they have met the child's need for an inclusive placement. However, a child transported some distance from home will again be prevented from forming relationships with other children from the local community. In addition, the parents may be denied normal opportunities to

13

meet other parents at the school gate and could well have real difficulty in getting into school on a regular basis, preventing the development of cooperative working practices.

Where additional specialist teaching and support staff are appointed to a resourced school, the class teacher may see no need to become involved with the child's educational programme. Although children with Down's Syndrome may spend much of the day in a mainstream class, they are likely to remain the responsibility of the resource provision teacher and his or her support assistants. If several special needs children are placed in the same resourced school, but in different classes, there is a tendency for them to be withdrawn and taught as a group for part of each day.

In some schools, with a special unit, they may be taught separately for much of the time, integrating with their peers only for non-academic subjects such as music or physical education (PE). A single specialist teacher, responsible for up to 15 children spread throughout the school, will find it extremely difficult to work with them all, unless such groupings are arranged, even with the support of one or two classroom assistants. While necessary for the effective deployment of staff, these groupings may not be in the best interests of the children.

If one considers the needs of young children with Down's Syndrome, it is difficult to see why they cannot be offered all the benefits of resourced provision in their local school. No evidence currently exists to show that children with Down's Syndrome gain academically from being taught alongside others with similar learning difficulties. In fact, the reverse is the case, as the stimulation and good models provided by more able children, accelerate their learning. Socially, primary aged children with Down's Syndrome appear to have few problems in making friends and being accepted by their peers.

On the other hand, the needs of the class teacher are often neglected when local placements are being arranged. The majority of primary teachers are well able to provide high-quality education for children with Down's Syndrome. However, it is important that they are offered appropriate levels of support and training, both before and after the child's arrival. In Denmark (Glaesel, 1997), teachers taking a child with significant difficulties are given:

- extra time to prepare lessons,
- a small bonus in addition to normal salary,
- a slightly reduced class size,
- an extra support person,
- access to training.

Although such inducements are rare in the UK, the package of support illustrated in Figure 2.3 is recommended and should be achievable in any mainstream school.

While a local mainstream school appears to be the most appropriate placement for most primary aged pupils with Down's Syndrome, the position may, in some cases, be somewhat different at secondary level. With an increasingly complex curriculum, taught by a range of subject specialists, the task of differentiation becomes more demanding. Targeted help from learning support teachers is often required to ensure maximum access for the student with Down's Syndrome. In some curriculum areas, the need for focused teaching on a withdrawal basis may increase and, at the same time, the importance of coordinating the student's overall programme of teaching and support becomes critical.

All these tasks can be performed by an effective team of Special Needs Coordinator (SENCO), learning support teachers, support assistants and pastoral staff in a local high school. Just such a team is described in the latest audio-tape from CSIE (Shaw, 1997). However, sufficient time must be allocated by senior management for planning, liaison and staff training. This is not always

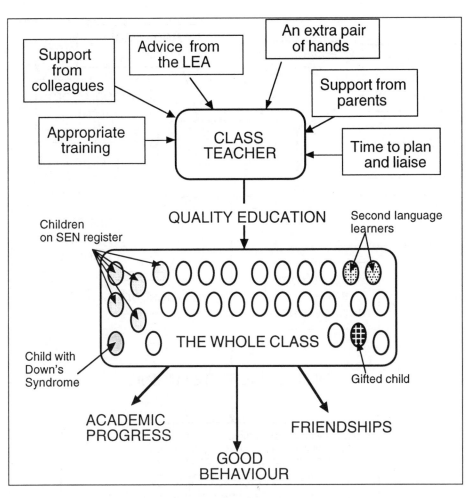

Figure 2.3 Supporting the teacher

possible without additional funding from the LEA. The focused or resourced school model provides one way in which these requirements can be met and expertise developed in the secondary sector. At the same time, it allows young people with Down's Syndrome to have social contact with others at a similar level of maturity.

Socialisation does not appear to be a problem at primary level, However, the teenage years often see normally developing students growing away from their learning disabled peers, leaving the child with Down's Syndrome socially isolated. In some instances, parents with placements in ordinary schools are choosing to supplement the mainstream diet with some time in a special school for just this reason. However, a focused school can provide the same opportunities without the need for the child to attend two different establishments. Although the parents of young people in focused schools often express concern about their children being separated from their friends in the local community, most are able to maintain local friendships made at primary level, by the use of community leisure facilities.

Ideally, all secondary schools should be additionally resourced. However, this is not likely to be a reality in the short term. One way of minimising the locational problems is to make all focused schools generic, rather than each specialising in one type of disability. Since it is largely the provision of additional staffing, a positive attitude of staff to students with disabilities and the availability of specialist resources that are most important, there seems no reason why a focused school should not be able to cater for the full range of special needs (see Figure 2.4). Rather than having one school resourced for

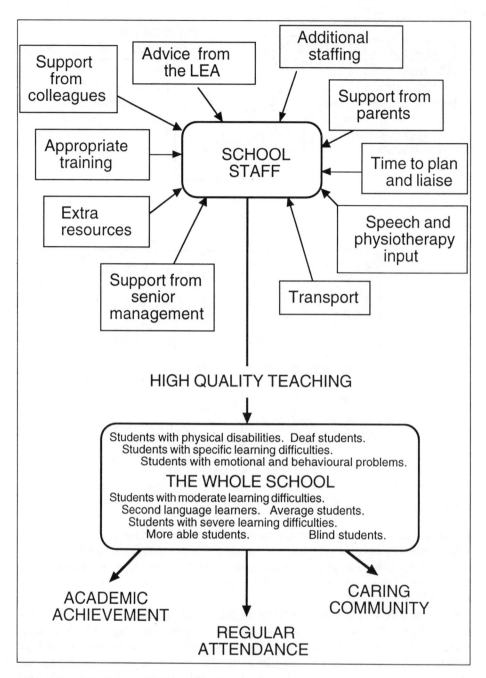

Figure 2.4 The focused high school

students with physical disabilities, one for those with hearing impairment, one for students with moderate, one for those with severe and one for those with specific learning difficulties, for example, the same population could be served by five generic focused schools. Parents would have a far wider choice and students should be able to find an additionally resourced school in their own neighbourhood, attended by at least some of their friends from primary school.

Outcomes of inclusive education

As Farrell (1997) notes, there is still relatively little research evidence comparing the performance of young people with Down's Syndrome in the mainstream with those in special schools. Because of the selective practices in some LEAs it is difficult to be sure that one is comparing like with like. Where parents have to fight to gain a mainstream place, it will be the children from the most supportive and better educated families who are successful. As research has shown, these are just the children who are also likely to be performing at a higher level.

Nevertheless, the research that does exist indicates that most children with Down's Syndrome do at least as well, if not better, in mainstream than in special schools. Studies comparing primary-aged children in mainstream and special schools, matched for ability, found those in mainstream did better on assessments of general reading ability (Lorenz *et al.*, 1985), reading comprehension and number (Casey *et al.*, 1988) and on a general academic index comprising teacher assessments of reading, writing and number skills (Sloper *et al.*, 1990).

Data on students of secondary age are even harder to come by and samples are much smaller and more restricted. Nevertheless, Sloper and Turner (1994) repeated their 1990 study when the students were aged from 11 to 17. They found that those in mainstream classes had higher academic scores than those in special schools. However, since they were also the most able, the least excitable and those with mothers who used a high proportion of practical coping strategies, it is not possible to attribute the apparent gains to placement alone, although it is clearly a significant factor. Overall, as Cunningham *et al.* (1998) note, the studies now available confirm that:

> Those children who are in integrated and mainstream classes have significantly higher scores on their academic attainments (although the difference is small). Also they do not have lower scores on the self-sufficiency skills – often given emphasis in special educational settings.

What studies have as yet been unable to tell us is whether children with Down's Syndrome in the mainstream are as well adjusted and have as high a level of self-esteem as those in special schools. Anecdotal evidence would suggest that the majority of children with Down's Syndrome are very happy in mainstream settings, particularly at primary level. In the secondary sector, Lincoln *et al.* (1992) report that the three students with Down's Syndrome in their study were all regular and enthusiastic school attenders. They all appeared happy in school and none had shown any signs of emotional distress. Where placements do break down, the main reasons given appear to relate to the difficulties experienced by the school, in differentiating the curriculum or managing the child's behaviour, rather than to problems experienced by the children.

Most commonly, children with Down's syndrome transfer to special education when they are due to change schools. The receiving school may be unwilling to accept the challenge or professionals may fear that the child will not cope. Rarely are trial placements offered. With little if any evidence upon which to base their decisions, professionals have tended to play safe and recommend the less 'risky' option of special school. However, where children have transferred, the new placements have in most cases turned out to be just as successful as the old ones. Parents aware of this trend are tending to reject separate infant and junior schools in favour of all-through primaries. Thus, as Cunningham *et al.* (1998) comment, in future years 'far more children with Down's Syndrome should remain successfully in mainstream schools than is the case at present'.

Chapter 3

Models of Support

Including the child in school life

Inclusive education for the child with Down's Syndrome has three main purposes:

- to foster learning by the provision of appropriate and challenging educational programmes
- to help establish age-appropriate patterns of behaviour
- to encourage the development of meaningful relationships with peers, that will extend beyond the school day.

Merely placing the child with Down's Syndrome in a mainstream as opposed to a special school is likely to expose them to a more demanding and broad ranging curriculum taught by staff with higher expectations. The Audit Commission (DfE 1992) commented that:

> The quality of pupils' learning in special schools was affected by a lack of pace in lessons. In addition there was a general absence of assessment and associated response to pupils' individual needs, and in some classes a low level of expectation for pupils.

The presence of normally developing peers should allow the child with Down's Syndrome to be presented with models of age-appropriate behaviour. In addition, relationships formed with children from the local community are more likely to lead to social contacts during the evening, at weekends or in the holidays, than those established with children bussed into school from a wide catchment area as would be the case were they attending a special school. Nevertheless, while these opportunities undoubtedly exist in a local mainstream school, there is no guarantee that they will be used to best effect.

Experience suggests that some children with Down's Syndrome are provided with an individualised curriculum, totally divorced from that offered to their peers. In some cases, this consists of skills, such as colour matching or sorting, that the child has already mastered at home. In others, the child is offered a programme quite inappropriate for his or her age, on the assumption, for example, that a six-year-old with Down's Syndrome will need to spend several hours a week playing in the nursery. Despite extensive research evidence to the contrary, some teachers are unable to accept that a child with Down's Syndrome can learn to read at much the same age as other children and so the child may be withdrawn during reading sessions or left to play in the home corner.

If the child has a full-time support assistant, there is the temptation for class teachers to hand over responsibility for the child's educational programme to the assistant, who may plan a pattern of work without reference to the class timetable. Children may spend much of their time working on a one-to-one basis with a support assistant and fail to benefit from the stimulation and models provided by the peer group. Further, they may be denied input from a trained teacher and opportunities to work cooperatively with others. Where LEA advisory teachers or outreach staff from a special school are actively involved in designing the child's Individual Education Plan (IEP), there is a danger that they see only the child and the support assistant, further increasing this isolation.

A child taught separately for most of the day will not be perceived as part of the class and, as a consequence, other children are less likely to socialise with him or her in school or in the local community. Where such a child is also supported by an adult at break and at lunchtime, opportunities for practising age-appropriate behaviours and forming relationships in a normal manner will be further reduced and the child can become socially isolated. This is common when staff or parents are particularly anxious about the child's safety. It is quite possible for supervision to be conducted from a distance, allowing the child to play, queue for dinner or line up to come into class, safely with all the other children. A child continually led by the hand may feel very secure and comfortable, but will never be accepted as a full member of the school community.

Even more difficulties can be caused by the practice, common in some LEAs, of keeping a child with Down's Syndrome back a year – or even more – in a desperate search for the elusive curriculum match. A recent survey, conducted by the author, suggests that while approximately 59 per cent of children with Down's Syndrome are currently placed with their own age group, some 34 per cent are with children a year younger, and around 7 per cent have been kept back two years. Not only will the children be confused and disheartened by the fact that all their friends are moving up without them, but the slow process of relationship building will have to start all over again.

Further, the hope that a child placed with a much younger class will be able to take part in normal lessons, without the need for special planning or differentiation, is rarely fulfilled. Nevertheless, in some instances, particularly where a child is summer-born, an extra year in nursery is recommended. However, once children start their formal schooling, they should, wherever possible, remain with the same peer group and move with them from one class to the next. While each case is obviously unique, the basic principles shown in Figure 3.1 are recommended to maximise the benefits of inclusive placement.

Planning an Individual Education Plan

In designing an IEP for a child with Down's Syndrome it is important to keep the reasons for inclusive placement in mind. To benefit from a challenging curriculum, good role models and opportunities to make friends, the child needs to participate as fully as possible in school and class activities. Before designing the IEP those involved should be familiar with what the rest of the class is likely to be doing throughout the day. While some slight modification to the class timetable may be required to accommodate the child with Down's Syndrome, it should not be necessary for major revisions to be made. With creative planning, by teachers and learning support assistants, the child with Down's Syndrome should be able to participate at an appropriate level in most normal activities.

The first stage of planning, therefore, involves listing those whole school or class activities in which the target child could take part, without close adult support (see Figure 3.2). In some cases an adequate level of supervision can be offered by the class teacher or by the child's friends. In others, an additional adult is required. However, support should be at a distance, with the aim of phasing it out as soon as possible. As the child progresses up the school, the total time devoted to largely unsupported activities should, ideally, increase as the child gains in skill and confidence and becomes more integrated with the class.

The next level of planning should focus on those activities or topics in which the child can participate, as long as additional adult support is available (see Figure 3.3). The key here is appropriate differentiation to allow the child access to the topic and an opportunity for real success. A good support assistant can be invaluable in guiding and supporting the child through the programme. However, it is essential that the class teacher retains ultimate responsibility for

1. Place children with their own age group or at most one year behind. Repeat the nursery year if necessary, but try not to hold children back once they are in Reception.

2. Make sure children take part in all school activities. Do not withdraw them during assembly or excuse them from lining up at dinner time.

3. Give children some time each day without close adult supervision. Give them space to make friends and learn by making mistakes.

4. As the class teacher, try to build a relationship with the child. Don't let the support assistant monopolise the child.

5. Encourage children to take part in most class activities alongside their peers. Let them work with more able children in a pair or a group.

6. Make sure the class teacher is involved in planning. Relate the child's IEP to the class programme.

7. Gradually decrease the intensity of support to build the child's ability to work independently and solve problems. Do not jump in too soon.

8. Teach basic class and school rules. Do not give the child special treatment.

9. Keep your expectations high but do not blame yourself if these children fall behind the rest of the class – they will. Nothing you do can make the Down's Syndrome or its consequences go away.

10. Get to know the child's parents and their philosophy. Learn all you can about Down's Syndrome but accept that each child is an individual with a unique pattern of strengths and weaknesses.

Figure 3.1 Tips for inclusive placement

designing the programme and monitoring the child's progress. Professional advice can be a real help, particularly where class teachers are taking on the challenge of teaching a child with Down's Syndrome for the first time. Nevertheless, outside 'experts' must not be allowed to take over, however tempting this may be to the hard-pressed class teacher.

Finally, attention needs to be paid to those areas of the curriculum which cannot be made accessible or relevant to each particular child with Down's Syndrome. In some situations, the most appropriate course of action is to use these times for specialised activities – e.g. the delivery of a speech therapy programme or word processing a piece of creative writing (see Figure 3.4). In others, the class lesson can be used as a setting in which social, fine-motor or communication skills can be practised – e.g helping the teacher give instructions, organising practical equipment or putting up a display of class work. Basic skills, such as one-to-one correspondence, may be achieved far more appropriately giving out apparatus in a technology lesson, than during maths, if the class is working, for example, on fractions.

While IEPs can take many forms, they should always spell out:

- the aim of each activity and the targets to be achieved
- ways in which the activity will be modified, to meet the needs of the child
- the teaching or support strategies that will be used (see Figure 3.5).

In-class support

Every child with Down's Syndrome in a mainstream school, should be able to take part in at least some activities with minimal support. However, for the majority of the day, tasks will need to be modified and adapted to ensure that they are relevant and appropriate. For much of the time, maximum benefit will only be obtained if the child has access to a classroom assistant or support teacher. A nation-wide survey recently carried out by the author indicates that 70 per cent of children with Down's Syndrome in mainstream schools are supported by a learning support assistant for more than 20 hours a week at primary level and for between 15 and 20 hours in the secondary sector.

At the opposite end of the scale, around 5 per cent of children are allocated 10 hours LSA support a week or even less. While this is frequently supplemented by teacher support at secondary level, such input is rare in the primary phase. Instead, primary schools may fund additional LSA hours from their own budgets or use volunteers to increase the amount of help available.

Clearly, there are individual students for whom only minimal support is required. However, the practice is not generally recommended. All children benefit from some time without direct support. On the other hand, it is not possible for a busy class teacher to deliver an appropriately flexible and differentiated curriculum on their own, without disadvantaging the rest of the class. In organising support for the student with Down's Syndrome, the class teacher should aim to:

- keep withdrawal to a minimum and give the child access to as much of the normal curriculum as possible
- encourage the child to become an independent learner
- foster cooperative working with other children in the class
- work directly with the children themselves, at least once a week, and ideally daily.

Child's name: Scott Daniels
D.o.b.: 1.3.92.
Class teacher: Trudy Matthews
Date of last review: 5.1.98.
Date of next review: 10.3.98.

UNSUPPORTED ACTIVITIES		
ACTIVITY	TARGETS	STRATEGIES
1. Hanging up coat in cloakroom.	(a) Removing coat without help. (b) Hanging it on correct peg.	(i) Mum to undo toggles. (ii) Picture on peg.
2. Going into assembly.	(a) Lining up with peers. (b) Moving in line into hall.	(i) Reminder from teacher. (ii) Best friend behind in line.
3. Break.	(a) Staying in playground.	(i) Reminder from teacher on duty. (ii) Smiley face sticker from class teacher.
4. Dinnertime.	(a) Collecting meal from counter. (b) Eating dinner before pudding.	(i) Tray with dinner only. (ii) Pudding given when dinner finished.
5. Storytime.	(a) Sitting still on floor. (b) Listening to story.	(i) Sitting near teacher. (ii) Ensuring can see pictures.

Figure 3.2 A model IEP (Part 1)

Child's name: Scott Daniels
D.o.b.: 1.3.92.
Class teacher: Trudy Matthews
Date of last review: 5.1.98.
Date of next review: 10.3.98.

SUPPORTED ACTIVITIES

ACTIVITY	TARGETS	STRATEGIES
1. News time.	(a) To underwrite one sentence in news book.	(i) Assistant to write down one sentence given by Scott (with help).
2. Model making.	(a) To cut out simple shapes	(i) Assistant to draw black line round shapes. (ii) Provide large-holed scissors.
3. Literacy hour.	(a) To read 10 new words from reading scheme. (b) To read book aloud with 90% accuracy.	(i) Assistant to test group on flash cards. (ii) Scott to read book individually to assistant.
4. Group work	(a) To take turns. (b) To co-operate on group task for 10 minutes.	(i) Daily session with 3 others. (ii) Assistant at same table. (iii) Different task each day.

Figure 3.3 A model IEP (Part 2)

Child's name: Scott Daniels
D.o.b.: 1.3.92.
Class teacher: Trudy Matthews
Date of last review: 5.1.98.
Date of next review: 10.3.98.

INDIVIDUAL ACTIVITIES

ACTIVITY	TARGETS	STRATEGIES
1. Language programme.	(a) To use 'in' 'on' and 'under'. (b) To use two words together.	(i) Withdrawal for last 10 mins. of maths. (ii) Furniture and games from Derbyshire Language Scheme.
2. Writing.	(a) To form letters correctly.	(i) While class doing free writing. (ii) 'Roll and write'+ sand tray.
3. Memory training.	(a) To remember simple message. (b) To deliver to teacher in another room.	(i) Twice each day, assistant to give Scott message and teach rehearsal. (ii) Reward if given correctly.

Figure 3.4 A model IEP (Part 3)

| Child's name: |
| D.o.b.: |
| Class teacher: |
| Date of last review: |
| Date of next review: |

ACTIVITY	TARGETS	STRATEGIES

Figure 3.5 A model IEP

These objectives are best met where class teacher and support staff see themselves as a team, working flexibly to meet the needs of the whole class. As Lorenz (1998) notes, a support assistant who is always at hand and who prompts the child continually or intervenes immediately the child is faced with a problem, will inhibit the development of independence. Far better is a situation where the assistant offers support only when needed and works regularly with other students who require help. Although some parents become very agitated when they find some of their child's hours being used to assist other children, this approach is likely to be far more beneficial in the long term than continual one-to-one support. It frees the class teacher to work directly with the child and gives the child opportunities to work with other people.

In some schools, particularly in the secondary sector, young people with Down's Syndrome are increasingly being supported by more than one assistant. This can work well where communication is good and support staff are placed in settings where their particular skills can be used to best effect. This approach, while still relatively uncommon, has several advantages:

● it avoids the unnaturally close relationship which sometimes develops between child and assistant
● it allows cover to be arranged more readily if one assistant is ill or on a training course, and
● it avoids the trauma caused to a child whose support assistant leaves.

In the author's survey, virtually all primary-aged pupils were being supported by one assistant. However, in the secondary sector, 32 per cent had two or three assistants, while 20 per cent were being supported by different assistants in different subject areas. In their study of ten inclusive secondary schools from five different LEAs, Lee and Henkhuzens (1996) recommended the attachment of support assistants to subject departments for the following reasons.

● It enables learning support assistants to become familiar with the subject area and the way in which each topic will be approached.
● It allows the assistants to feel more confident in their ability to support students appropriately, particularly where it is possible to place assistants in subject areas where they already have confidence, expertise or interest.
● It increases opportunities for assistants and subject staff to work together to produce a bank of appropriate materials.

In primary schools where there is more than one child receiving support, changing the support assistant, as well as the teacher, when the child moves classes can be a useful strategy, although one that is rarely used. Not only does this encourage the new teacher to take a personal interest in the child with Down's Syndrome, but it prevents the assistant and child becoming too close. Where the assistant is able to remain with the same teacher, rather than the same child, joint working practices can be developed over time to the benefit of all. However, in many schools this is not possible as their funding only permits them to employ one support assistant. Nevertheless, there is still a lot that can be done to prevent difficulties when a school is aware of the potential pitfalls.

Experience suggests that children who keep the same assistant for years are at risk of being left in their care as the support assistant is seen as the person who knows the child best. Recent survey data indicate that in 28 per cent of cases primary aged children with Down's Syndrome are taught by their class teacher less than once a week. Almost all direct teaching is carried out by support assistants. Yet we know that over half the learning support assistants involved have no formal qualifications, nor have they received any training in the teaching of children with Down's Syndrome. As the Green Paper (DfEE 1997b) notes: 'The reliance which many schools place on LSAs makes training and career development essential. But training opportunities and patterns of employment are patchy and need to be improved if we are to realise the full potential of their contribution'

An assistant who has worked almost exclusively with the same child for a long time may be reluctant to let go and may be unwilling to work with other children in the class, even if this is in the target child's best interest. While parents and professionals should undoubtedly be fighting to maintain an adequate level of support for every child with Down's Syndrome, they should be equally vigilant and object just as strongly where children are being over-supported. Current research suggests that in 53 per cent of cases the child's support assistant sits next to him or her for most of the time, occasionally or never working with other children in the class. Hopefully, as teachers get more confident in teaching students with Down's Syndrome and learn to work more flexibly with support staff, the picture will change.

Most schools, quite rightly, emphasise the need to provide an adequate level of support for the child. However, they often fail to recognise or acknowledge the support needs of their staff. Parents and teachers should insist that time is provided for support assistants and teachers to plan their work. SENCOs, whose responsibility it is to manage the support staff, should ensure that they are given sufficient time away from their normal teaching duties to carry out this essential function.

Although non-contact time is provided in nearly two-thirds of high schools, when teachers and assistants can discuss their respective roles, less than a third of primary support assistants are given paid planning time. Undoubtedly some will stay behind after school or give up their lunch break to discuss the needs of the children they support. However, it seems unreasonable for schools to take advantage of the goodwill of such poorly paid staff. The solution lies in the hands of LEAs who should recognise the importance of planning and build it into the provision on the child's statement.

Support in the secondary school

In the primary school there is little choice for the class teacher, other than to involve the child in normal classroom activities or alternatively, to ask the support assistant to work with them individually or in a small group. At secondary level there are many more possible options (see Figure 3.6).

Preliminary findings from a survey carried out by the author suggest that most secondary-aged students with Down's Syndrome are taught in mixed-ability classes for at least part of the week. Approximately half of the students received some additional in-class support from a learning support teacher in maths, English or French, while around 58 per cent were withdrawn for individual or small group help at least once a week. Although most students with Down's Syndrome spend some time in bottom sets, one young man has been placed in the third of four sets to avoid the disaffected and troublesome pupils often found in lower achieving groups. This is particularly pertinent for students with Down's Syndrome who frequently mimic the behaviour of their peers. As Lee and Henkhuzens (1996) note:

> If you have a group of pupils with learning difficulties (and maybe associated behavioural difficulties) all together, there are no positive role models available, the teacher may be the only source of ideas and information, and the group may be perceived as difficult to teach.

None of the primary-aged students in the study were disapplied from the National Curriculum, although a small percentage of those in secondary schools were disapplied from modern languages. In some schools, the provision of a Learning Support option at Key Stage 4 allowed additional time to be given to basic skills or complementary studies. When support staff are used, be they teachers or support assistants, it is important that all concerned are clear about their role. They should be there, primarily, to assist the student (see Figure 3.7).

27

- The student can work as a member of a mixed-ability class, supported by the subject teacher alone, by a support teacher or by a support assistant.

- The student can work as a member of a lower set containing fewer students, either with or without additional support.

- The student can work in a small group of lower ability children supported by an additional member of staff within a mixed ability classroom.

- The student can be supported individually, carrying out his or her own special work within the classroom situation.

- The student can be withdrawn in a group, taught by a learning support teacher.

- The student can be withdrawn individually by a teacher, a therapist or a support assistant for counselling or for the delivery of a specialised intervention programme.

Figure 3.6 Models of support in the high school

However, they also have a role to play in supporting the subject teacher (see Figure 3.8).

None of these roles is mutually exclusive. While some are best carried out by subject specialists, others are better performed by learning support teachers with additional skills in differentiation, counselling or special needs teaching. Many of the roles can be carried out equally well by teachers or support assistants. However, schools must ensure that staff without teaching qualifications are not asked to plan work or teach students on a withdrawal basis unless they are under the direct supervision of the class teacher. On the other hand, using teachers for general in-class support may be a poor use of scarce resources (Margerison, 1997).

One key aim of support at secondary level must be to increase students' independence and progressively reduce their need for adult assistance. An adult accompanying a primary-aged child around the school building is accepted as fairly normal practice. However, adults do not generally follow secondary-aged students from one class to the next. In developing independence and improving organisational skills, the commonly used homework diary or planner can be a real help, not only to the student but also to parents who are no longer able to see school staff informally on a daily basis. Lists of equipment or sports kit can be written down and students encouraged to check their books each evening before preparing their school bags for the next day. Maps of the school building can be included, to help students find their way around, as well as the names of teaching and non-teaching staff with whom they may come into contact.

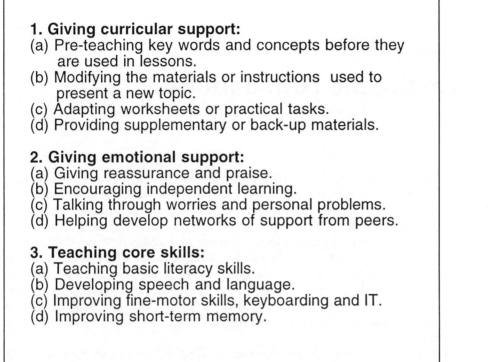

1. Giving curricular support:
(a) Pre-teaching key words and concepts before they are used in lessons.
(b) Modifying the materials or instructions used to present a new topic.
(c) Adapting worksheets or practical tasks.
(d) Providing supplementary or back-up materials.

2. Giving emotional support:
(a) Giving reassurance and praise.
(b) Encouraging independent learning.
(c) Talking through worries and personal problems.
(d) Helping develop networks of support from peers.

3. Teaching core skills:
(a) Teaching basic literacy skills.
(b) Developing speech and language.
(c) Improving fine-motor skills, keyboarding and IT.
(d) Improving short-term memory.

Figure 3.7 Supporting the student

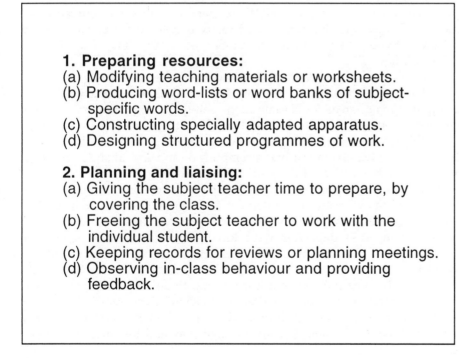

1. Preparing resources:
(a) Modifying teaching materials or worksheets.
(b) Producing word-lists or word banks of subject-specific words.
(c) Constructing specially adapted apparatus.
(d) Designing structured programmes of work.

2. Planning and liaising:
(a) Giving the subject teacher time to prepare, by covering the class.
(b) Freeing the subject teacher to work with the individual student.
(c) Keeping records for reviews or planning meetings.
(d) Observing in-class behaviour and providing feedback.

Figure 3.8 Supporting the teacher

Chapter 4
Laying the Foundations

Early
intervention

By the time children with Down's Syndrome reach school, they are likely to have been receiving input from a range of professionals for some time. Most will have been referred to a local Child Development Centre or equivalent hospital service, where they will be screened for medical problems and offered the opportunity to receive physiotherapy. Parents will generally have been shown how to work with their child at home, exercising weak muscles and encouraging early learning skills. They may also have received input from a speech therapist and introduced to a signing system such as Makaton. In many areas of the country, children with Down's Syndrome and their families will have been offered weekly support from a Portage Service or other form of early intervention.

From the onset of these programmes in Great Britain in the 1970s, children with Down's Syndrome have always comprised a very large proportion of their case loads. The reasons for this seem fairly obvious. For instance, the syndrome is easily identified at birth and thus referrals can be made early. Diagnosis is rarely contentious and so there are none of the reservations about labelling felt by professionals in other conditions. While there are still some differences in opinion as to long-term gains in measured ability, there is no doubt that children with Down's Syndrome and their families benefit, in a variety of ways, from early intervention.

On entry to school, young children who have been receiving Portage input are likely to be quite skilled and to be familiar with a range of structured tasks covering the main areas of socialisation, self-help, cognitive, motor and language development. They will be used to sitting still for short periods of time and complying with instructions in a one-to-one setting. They will be familiar with the use of demonstration and prompting – and are likely to respond positively to praise on successful completion of a task.

However, it is also important for schools to be aware of some of the problems that can be caused by certain early intervention programmes. 'Switching out' or 'learned helplessness', as Wishart (1996) terms them, can cause real problems in school – as can adult dependency. Children who have become reliant on structured input, regular prompting and high levels of social reinforcement, are likely to benefit less from inclusive placement than those who have been encouraged to become independent learners and to develop cooperative play skills. Nevertheless, most young children with Down's Syndrome will have no difficulty in adapting to the less structured setting of the nursery or reception class and will be readily able to learn through play and imitation, like other children.

Teachers will find that parents who have been involved in Portage will be more aware of their child's development than the average parent and will be used to playing an active part in their child's education. This can cause tensions between home and school if the respective roles of teacher and parent are not established clearly from the onset. However, where schools are able to value parental skills and commitment, and work positively with them, the benefits are enormous, both to the child and to the school as a whole. Information and advice from the child's Portage worker can also be of considerable help in the first few months. In some LEAs, home visitors will come into school during the first term, helping the child and family to adjust, and dealing with concerns expressed by the school staff. This gradual handing-over is a practice that should be encouraged, as much valuable information gained by preschool services never gets into schools.

Motor skills

By the age of three years, most young children with Down's Syndrome will be walking independently. While some will be quite agile, others will still be somewhat unsteady and have difficulty on stairs or with playground equipment. Children of nursery or reception age are, therefore, likely to need help and encouragement in developing a range of motor skills – including pedalling a tricycle, throwing and catching a ball, running and jumping. A nursery is an ideal setting in which children can be introduced to a wide range of physical activities, both indoors and outside. The presence of other children obviously enjoying active play may encourage a rather apprehensive or lethargic youngster to try out an activity for the first time or to practise an emergent skill. This is as true for the child with Down's Syndrome as it is for all other children.

However, care must be taken to ensure that the child is not overwhelmed or knocked over by boisterous peers. Conversely, other children should be actively discouraged from treating children with Down's Syndrome as babies, leading them everywhere by the hand or pushing them around in a pram. Although some children may tolerate or even enjoy this, it will do nothing to encourage their participation in the full range of activities. It also gives unhelpful messages to staff, parents and children as to the role that the child with Down's Syndrome is expected to play.

In other cases it may lead children to become aggressive, biting or kicking in an attempt to assert their independence. Such behaviour, while worrying, tends to pass as the other children learn to accept the child with Down's Syndrome as an equal. Indoors, a variety of enjoyable group activities can be incorporated into the curriculum to encourage the child with Down's Syndrome to improve motor skills alongside normally developing peers. Cooperative games using music and actions can be particularly effective with young children who may have limited language skills.

Not only can poor muscle tone give rise to delays in gross-motor development, but also it has an effect on the acquisition of fine-motor skills. Most young children with Down's Syndrome possess excellent visual perceptual abilities. However, low muscle tone combined with the slack ligaments and short stubby fingers of the condition, lead to marked clumsiness in eye–hand coordination. Extensive practice will therefore be required if the child is to develop handwriting and other important school-related skills.

In the early years, some specialised or modified equipment such as inset puzzles with large knobs, may be useful. However, it is by no means essential. In some areas, expensive equipment can be borrowed from a helpful toy library or special school. Nevertheless, most early years settings will have access to a range of appropriate materials – e.g. large plastic cotton reels for threading. Fat crayons and stubby paintbrushes may be easier for the child to handle than slimmer versions. These should be readily available at minimal cost and should prove of value to a number of other children.

Cutting out is a skill that many children find difficult to acquire, but it is particularly problematic for most youngsters with Down's Syndrome. Here, specially adapted scissors available in most educational catalogues can be invaluable. These come in a variety of forms including some with double

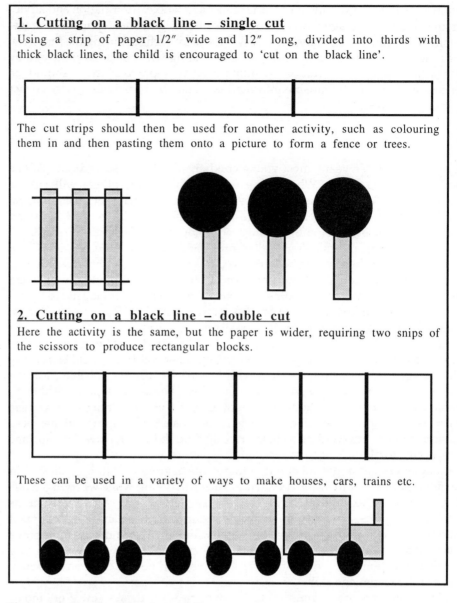

Figure 4.1 Developing scissor skills

handles, which enable an adult to model the correct finger movements. The correct sensations are experienced by the child, who is gradually allowed to take over control.

Others scissors with a spring handle require only slight pressure to produce a cutting movement. While very successful early on, it is unwise to allow children to rely on this form of equipment for too long, as they will find it increasingly difficult to adapt to normal scissors. Particularly useful are those with elongated finger holes that allow the child to place both first and second fingers in the same hole, for extra pressure. An excellent little book *Diagnosing and Teaching Scissor Skills* (published in 1976, but now unfortunately out of print), suggests the progression of activities outlined Figures 4.1 and 4.2.

3. Cutting out shapes

Draw a square in the centre of a sheet of paper with a thick black pen. Colour it in and draw a green line from one corner of the shape to the edge of the paper. This will need to be on the right hand side for the right-handed child and on the left for the left-hander.

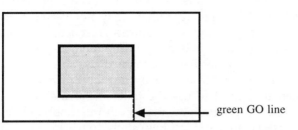

green GO line

This GO line will help the child get their scissors to the shape, to start cutting it out. However, they may still need to be shown how to turn the paper round with their non-cutting hand when they get to a corner.

After a square, the child should progress to cutting out triangles, diamonds and circles. In time, the green GO line should no longer be necessary. The shapes produced can be stuck onto a prepared background or combined to make more complex designs such as a house or a kite.

4. Cutting out designs

Encourage the child to cut out shapes or pictures from catalogues or magazines. Start by outlining each shape with a black pen and adding a green GO line, but aim to phase these out as soon as the child becomes more confident.

At any of the above stages, a child having a particular difficulty can be helped by sticking card to the back of the paper, between the cutting lines. This will discourage cutting away from the line.

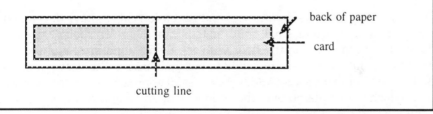

back of paper

card

cutting line

Figure 4.2 Developing scissor skills – 2

On starting in the Nursery or Reception class, many young children with Down's Syndrome will not be as independent in caring for themselves as their peers. Although there is no reason why Down's Syndrome in itself should cause any particular problem in toilet training, children with Down's Syndrome can also be affected by unrelated disorders such as Hirschprung's disease, which interferes with the functioning of the bowel. Such conditions should have been identified before the child starts school. However, it is worth inquiring about possible medical causes if normal toiletting patterns cannot be established by the end of the Reception year.

In most children with Down's Syndrome, the development of self-help skills is likely to be affected by their general delay. Although a reasonable degree of independence should be achieved in the early years, it would be inappropriate to expect a child functioning below a two-year level overall to be consistently clean and dry, to be dressing themselves unaided or to be able to use a knife and

Self-help skills

fork. Where parents are getting worried about an apparent lack of progress in these areas, the use of a developmental checklist, provided by the educational psychologist or health visitor, should help to allay their anxieties.

In some cases, although the child is sufficiently mature, parents or carers may have found it difficult to establish age-appropriate routines of feeding, dressing or toiletting on their own. Some families may need support in overcoming their child's reluctance to cooperate. Others may not yet be ready to allow their 'special baby' to grow up and will require a great deal of encouragement.

Children who have always had liquidised food, may not know how to chew or use a fork and may not have developed the ability to control their bowel movements. Children who are always in nappies may not have learned to indicate when they need to use the toilet. Nevertheless, in most instances a consistently applied programme, used both in school and at home, should be effective in establishing basic self-help skills. In teaching independence skills, it is important that schools select appropriate times and settings. Teaching the child to undress for PE is likely to be more meaningful, and therefore more productive, than setting aside ten minutes each morning to work on a dressing programme.

The model provided by the other children is also an important resource. Most young children with Down's Syndrome want to be the same as everyone else and so will be keen to copy what the others are doing. Other children will often be the best teachers and in helping will establish relationships away from direct adult supervision. No special techniques are required to teach self-help skills to young children with Down's Syndrome. However, the following principles will work in most situations.

- Break the task down into small steps.
- Give clear simple instructions.
- Demonstrate what is required by using another child as a model.
- Give regular practice in an appropriate setting.
- Give the child time to process information before responding.
- Use praise consistently and lavishly,

Over the years, teachers in nurseries and Reception classes have developed a variety of ways of teaching small children to put on their own coats. These have included laying the coat on the floor with the lining uppermost and the neck nearest to the child. Children are taught to put their arms in the sleeves and then flick the coat over their heads. Another successful approach, is to use a coat with a hood which is first placed over the child's head, making it relatively easy for the child to find the correct arm holes and slip the coat on.

Many problems with dressing can be overcome by encouraging parents to select trouble-free clothes with elastic waists or Velcro fastenings, rather than buttons or laces. In the early years at least, it is more important for the child to be able to go to the toilet independently and dress after PE or swimming, than to be able to cope with difficult fastenings. More advanced skills are probably better taught in the home, where there is more time and less pressure to conform.

Language development

Delays in both the production and the comprehension of spoken language are the norm in young children with Down's Syndrome. As with all other skills, the degree of delay differs widely from one child to another. Rondal (1996) suggests that a baby with Down's Syndrome is less responsive to his or her mother's verbal stimulation than other children of the same age. Children with Down's Syndrome tend to take the initiative less often and are slow to develop essential turn-taking skills. Kumin (1994) also notes the influence on language development of a whole range of other factors including: repeated middle-ear infections, fluctuating hearing loss, low muscle tone, an oral cavity that is relatively small, over- or under-sensitivities to touch in and around the mouth, and general cognitive delay.

The physical consequences of Down's Syndrome can affect the intelligibility of speech, particularly the articulation of sounds, the fluency of speech, the sequencing of speech sounds and their quality and tone. While they make speaking more difficult and frustrating, these problems need not prevent effective communication. Most young children with Down's Syndrome are eager to communicate and naturally use a range of gestures and facial expressions. Levels of language understanding are often significantly greater than the child's skills in speech production. Children with Down's Syndrome also seem to be particularly adept at learning to sign. This ability, if shared with the adults and children around them, can significantly reduce frustration and allow time for speech to develop naturally alongside the sign language. In a recent survey of 13 primary-aged children with Down's Syndrome attending mainstream schools in South Devon (Beadman, 1997), it was noted that:

> Most children relied on Makaton as their main means of communication when they first started school. Generally verbal communication was sufficiently developed by the time the child was seven years old for signing to be dropped, although one child relied totally on signing at this age.

Following on from the pioneering work of Pat le Provost (1986), most speech and language therapists offer parents access to a signing system such as Makaton or Signalong, around two years of age. However, not all accept this as some parents still hold the largely unfounded belief that signing will delay speech development. Others fear that signing will make their child appear more 'handicapped'. Generally, the introduction of signing after the child reaches school age is not recommended as, by then, the child will have developed alternative forms of communication. However, normally developing children and school staff can be successfully introduced to signing at any stage and their ability to communicate with the signing child will greatly enhance opportunities for communication, as well as extending their own skill repertoire. In visiting schools for her evaluation, Jane Beadman (1997) comments that:

> Staff have availed themselves of training opportunities in Makaton made available via speech therapists and, sometimes, parents. They have been diligent and imaginative in their use of signing with the class group and with the individual child. In each class where signing was the main form of communication for the child with Down's Syndrome, there were regular periods in each day when the teacher signed to the whole class, and the rest of the class members were proficient in the basic signs – and enjoyed the sessions. Some classes were outstanding in their signing ability.

A range of videos combining sign and speech is now available in the high street for use in the early years. These videos provide a novel addition to the more usual school or nursery resources.

Despite significant delays, the stages of language acquisition appear to be largely the same in children with Down's Syndrome as in the normally developing population. Nevertheless, there are particular sticking points. The single word stage tends to be extended, often beyond the age of five or six. Yet these children can still ask or answer questions, make requests and give commands. To encourage the development of telegraphic speech, with two or more words strung together, it is important that adults avoid the use of closed questions which demand only a single word answer. It is also imperative that the children are given time to think before responding. Difficulties in auditory processing and memory, characteristic of children with Down's Syndrome, mean that they will take longer than other children to process and understand what is said to them, and even longer to find and organise the words required to make an appropriate response.

Despite the belief of many people that exposure to verbally fluent peers would, in itself, enhance language skills in young children with Down's Syndrome, research evidence fails to support this view. A recent study by Philps (1993), found that without structured intervention, children in mainstream settings were disadvantaged. If the gap between the language level of the target child and the peer group is too great, the child will be discouraged and communicate less. However, if situations are engineered in which the child is allowed to take the lead – e.g. by playing teacher or instructing others – then skills will be practised and will develop.

Improving memory

Children with Down's Syndrome are known to have a particularly poor short-term memory. Work by a variety of authors, however, has confirmed that they perform significantly better on tasks involving the processing and recall of visually presented material than on listening tasks. This applies whether they are expected to give a verbal response or to respond by performing an action. One explanation for this phenomenon may lie in the fact that the nerve fibres carrying auditory information develop their protective myelin sheath later in development than the visual nerves. As a consequence, they are more likely to be damaged or to function imperfectly if development is incomplete. Another set of theories looks to the behaviour of young children with Down's Syndrome and the difficulties they show in language-related tasks.

As children develop, they extend the range of their short-term listening memory by using techniques that help them retain, and subsequently recall, an increasing number of items. The first of these is rehearsal, by which the child repeats information sub-vocally, until it is required. Work by MacKenzie and Hulme (1992) suggests that children with Down's Syndrome lack this silent speech, which most children develop at around four years of age. However, this is a technique that can be taught very effectively and can be generalised to a variety of situations. Once children understand about rehearsal, they appear to be more able to remember telephone numbers or deliver messages. Further research, though, has indicated that the technique requires regular practice if the benefits are to be maintained.

Comblain (1994) used a training technique with teenagers that initially involved showing and naming a series of pictures in a fixed sequence. Later, the pictures were removed and the young people encouraged to repeat and then rehearse the names without any visual clue. This approach appears to be more effective than the use of verbally presented items such as word lists on their own. Along much the same lines, Broadley (1994) developed a range of training materials including a 'windows' device consisting of a cardboard strip with cut-out windows, behind which strips of pictures could be inserted. Although effective, it required the provision of a whole range of different picture strips to avoid the children becoming bored. She has, therefore, designed a more flexible system which should be of use to teachers and support assistants (see Figure 4.3).

This consists of a row of plastic pockets into which individual picture cards can be inserted. Not only can the sequence be varied in length, depending on the ability of the child, but also an infinite variety of different sequences can be created with minimal effort, once a reasonable number of pictures or photographs have been collected together. The fitting of an opaque flap over each pocket increases the versatility of the equipment, as pictures can be shown and then hidden while the child tries to remember what the item was. By lifting the flap briefly, children can peep to provide a prompt or check their answers. Regular short sessions with these materials, either in the classroom or on a

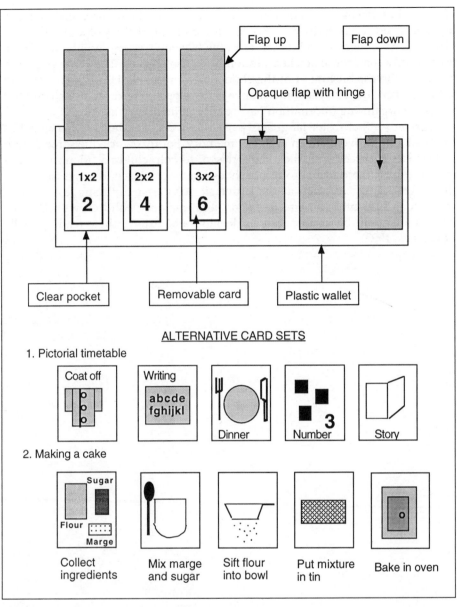

Figure 4.3 Memory training pockets

withdrawal basis, appear to be a particularly effective way of increasing the memory span of children with Down's Syndrome.

In addition to this structured training, students should be encouraged to practise using rehearsal techniques – e.g. by being given messages to deliver or verbal instructions to follow. The child should initially be taught to repeat the instructions out loud, while taking the message or carrying out the task, and later encouraged to speak more and more quietly, until the words are rehearsed silently. In school, a range of techniques can be used to compensate for the children's poorly developed listening memories. Pictorial timetables, developed originally for children with autistic spectrum disorders, can be very useful for the young child with Down's Syndrome. Here again the plastic memory pockets could be used, this time containing pictures of the activities or tasks to be completed, arranged in the correct order. Once an activity is finished, its picture can be removed and children encouraged to talk about what they will be doing next.

To supplement training in rehearsal techniques, Broadley has investigated the teaching of a second memory-building skill she terms 'organisation', by which the normally developing child learns to categorise items and group them together to aid recall. Individual books, stored on the shelves of a library, with related items alongside each other, as in the 'Dewey' system, will be found far more readily than those stacked randomly on the shelves. The same principle applies in the establishment of the child's memory bank. Unfortunately, most children with Down's Syndrome are late in developing concepts and so find the process of organising information particularly difficult.

Programmes that foster language, particularly concept development, will in turn lead to improvements in auditory memory. For this work, the same plastic pockets can be used, with their flaps raised, to help children 'identify all the animals', 'pick the odd one out' or 'choose pairs of objects that go together'. More significantly, research at the University of Portsmouth suggests that to establish and maintain an effective short-term memory, children with Down's Syndrome should be encouraged to develop and extend their reading skills (Laws *et al.*, 1995).

Chapter 5

Differentiating the Curriculum

With a few notable exceptions, children with Down's Syndrome are most unlikely to be able to access the National Curriculum at the same level as their peers. Further, the gap between their level of attainment and that of the rest of the class is almost certain to increase as they move through the school. This is a fact of life that is not the fault of the school or of the child. Once teachers accept the inevitability of this process and stop feeling guilty or that they have failed, then real progress can be made.

In modifying their programmes of study, teachers need to remember that the National Curriculum goes down to Level 1 and below. It is, therefore, unnecessary to consider disapplying a child with Down's Syndrome from any aspect of it. Evidence from schools and parents confirms the fact that Welsh children with Down's Syndrome are often bilingual, while others can learn to speak French or German very successfully, although these still tend to be the curriculum areas from which secondary-aged students with Down's Syndrome are most commonly withdrawn.

Further, it is not necessary for any student to work within the appropriate Key Stage. What is required is an assessment of the child and the level at which he or she is currently functioning. The teacher should then be able to select relevant National Curriculum targets that can be incorporated into the child's programme. A creative teacher with knowledge of the subject area should be able to incorporate Level 1 targets into a Level 3–4 programme of study, or targets from Level 2 into a topic designed for students at Levels 5–6.

In differentiating a topic or class lesson, a model of concentric circles can be a useful starting point (see Figure 5.1). Two or three key concepts or skills are selected from the topic, which the teacher would expect all students, including the pupil with Down's Syndrome, to have acquired at the end of the lesson. These might be fundamental principles such as:

- light is made up of waves
- the English alphabet contains 26 letters
- rivers flow downhill

or they might be skills such as:

- the ability to draw a diagram
- the ability to measure a line using a ruler
- the ability to answer a simple question in French.

These items are placed in the centre of the model. The next circle consists of items which, the teacher hopes, the majority of the class will understand or be able to complete successfully by the end of the lesson. As further circles are drawn on the diagram, the percentage of the class expected to achieve them will decrease. Finally, there will be aspects of the topic that would be attained only by the most able or the most diligent (see Figure 5.2).

In some lessons the majority of students would be expected, in time, to progress from the centre to the outer circles of the model. In others, the circles would represent different levels in the National Curriculum for children of different abilities. Rather than designing a series of separate parallel activities

Principles of differentiation

39

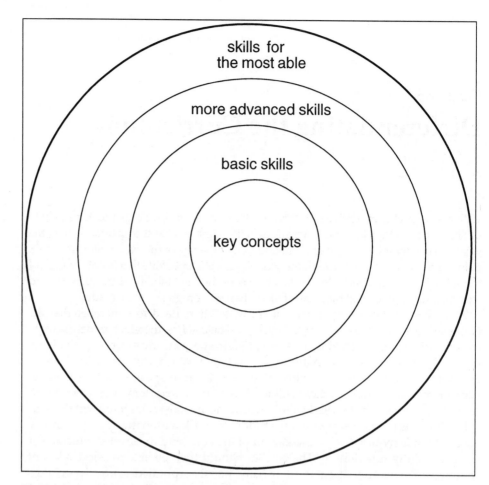

Figure 5.1 A concentric model for differentiation

around the same topic to accommodate students of different ability or aptitude, this concentric model allows the teacher to teach the class as a whole. Using this model, teachers have been surprised how capable some pupils with Down's Syndrome have turned out to be, when motivated by the desire to keep up with the rest of the class. On the other hand, a student who is struggling, can take the whole lesson to consolidate the items in the centre of the circle, without feeling a failure or having to be taken out to do something else entirely.

One way in which students can be given access to more demanding aspects of a topic is by pre-teaching, in school or at home. Stainback *et al.* (1996) describe a classroom where the teacher used the first 15 minutes of each day for news. Each student was asked to report to the class on a news story he or she had seen on the television or read in the newspaper the previous evening. To enable one student with severe learning difficulties to participate, the teacher asked his mother to coach him on a news story each evening. From that point he always had something to say when the teacher asked for volunteers. While prompting from classmates or the teacher was often necessary, the student gradually became an active participant in the class.

Effective teaching approaches

Having planned a series of appropriately differentiated lessons, the class teacher then needs to give some thought to the way in which new ideas can be communicated most effectively to the child with Down's Syndrome. In many cases, no attempt is made by class teachers to adapt their mode of presentation. Instead, the responsibility is handed over to the support assistant who is

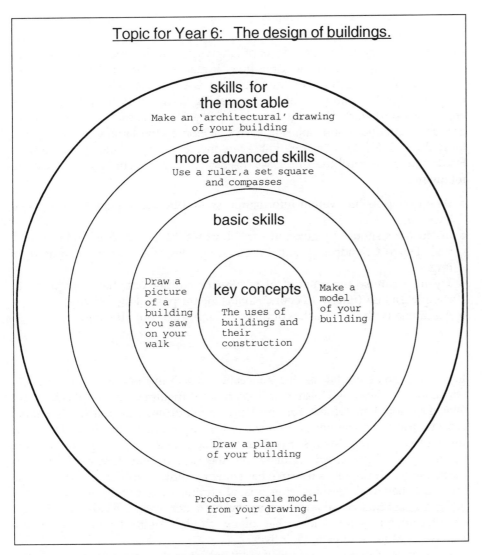

Figure labels within the diagram:

Topic for Year 6: The design of buildings.

skills for
the most able
Make an 'architectural' drawing
of your building

more advanced skills
Use a ruler, a set square
and compasses

basic skills

Draw a
picture
of a
building
you saw
on your
walk

key concepts

The uses of
buildings and
their
construction

Make a
model
of your
building

Draw a plan
of your building

Produce a scale model
from your drawing

Figure 5.2 A concentric model for differentiation

expected to translate or interpret the teacher's instructions. In some circumstances this approach can work well. However, it invariably means that:

- the child is totally dependent on his or her support assistant whenever new information is given
- the assistant is tied to the target child and so has no time to help others
- there is no direct communication between the class teacher and the child with Down's Syndrome
- the child sees no need to pay attention to the teacher
- the other children perceive the child with Down's Syndrome as different and dependent.

Far better is a situation in which the class teacher simplifies and modifies the way in which the lesson is presented to the class as a whole. We know that students with Down's Syndrome are likely to have more difficulty than most of their peers in processing and retaining verbal information. However, they will not be alone. In practice, many teachers have found that the adaptations made to assist the child with Down's Syndrome also benefit other pupils.

In some circumstances, the level of modification required is so great that the resulting language is inappropriate for the rest of the class. In such cases it is better that the teacher gives instructions in the normal way and then summarises the main points for the child with Down's Syndrome. This will act as a memory boost for any other children who have learning difficulties or who are not listening, without diluting the level of language to which the majority of class members are exposed. At the same time, it makes it clear that the child with Down's Syndrome is part of the class and is expected to listen along with everyone else. This can be reinforced by asking questions of the class members before they start work. Techniques such as first addressing each child by name to gain their attention, and tailoring each question to the language level of the individual child, can ensure that everyone, even the child with Down's Syndrome, can contribute to a class discussion. Other techniques include the following.

- Wherever possible, verbal information should be accompanied by a visual back-up.
- Instructions should be given in very short blocks. Never overload the child with Down's Syndrome with information; they will just get confused or forget.
- Try to minimise the amount of writing or cutting out that is required to complete a task (unless, of course, that is the purpose of the activity).
- Additionally, the approaches outlined in Figure 5.3 could be tried.

Using IT in the classroom

In recent years, there has been a noticeable growth in the use of computers in education, not least by children with learning difficulties. As Bob Black, South West Development Officer for the Down's Syndrome Association (personal communication) comments, a number of features make them especially useful for children with Down's Syndrome. When using a computer, all the information is presented visually on the screen and keyboard. This is particularly helpful for, as research has shown, children with Down's Syndrome are much better at learning from visual stimuli than purely auditorily. The advantages of this visual approach are even greater when the child has the sort of intermittent hearing loss that many children with Down's Syndrome experience at some stage in their lives.

A computer can overcome specific difficulties such as the fine-motor control required for handwriting, and allow the child to produce well-presented and legible work, possibly for the first time. Work can be drafted and redrafted several times over a lengthy period of time, thus overcoming problems of limited concentration span or poor motivation. Computers can provide a highly organised working environment in which the child can be in complete control, regardless of language or communication difficulties. Activities can be finely graded so that the child progresses gradually from easy to harder tasks without realising and switching off.

The computer allows children with Down's Syndrome to dictate their own pace for working. This in itself is advantageous in the development of independence. Further, experience suggests that children often keep their attention to task for longer periods when using computers than with traditional pencil and paper oriented work. Since many programs are both straightforward and self-motivating, it is often possible to leave the child using the computer for considerable periods of time, without adult support. Even higher levels of satisfaction can be achieved with multimedia presentations using speech, video, photographs and animation on CD-ROM. The National Curriculum Council identified five categories of benefits of information technology (IT) for children with special educational needs, as outlined below:

- heightened motivation
- opportunities to work in small groups

Use pictures on the wall, overhead projector slides or even drawings on the board, to illustrate your main points.

Encourage a support assistant who can draw, to illustrate your ideas with cartoons on a flip chart or white board.

Bring in examples of objects you are talking about for children to look at.

Demonstrate exactly what you want the children to do.

Use volunteers from the class to model good practice.

Summarise instructions in a written list, which remains on view.

Break tasks into a series of short steps.

Write each step, illustrated where appropriate, on a separate card, which children can keep on their table as a reminder.

Use the child's support assistant to help him or her rehearse the instructions and discuss exactly what is required of them.

Encourage the support assistant to move away, once it is clear that the child knows what to do, and monitor from a distance.

Only give out the next card when the first task is completed.

Ask children what should come next before telling them.

Let the child underline or ring the correct response.

Let the child tell his or her answer to another child who can record it for them.

Give them words or numbers on a roll of stickers to pull off and stick in their book.

Let them record their answers on a tape recorder or dictaphone.

Teach basic word processing skills or let them use a concept keyboard to encourage free writing.

Where appropriate, have models etc. cut out ready for assembly.

Figure 5.3 Effective teaching approaches

- improvements in accuracy and appearance of work
- better access to information
- the development of creativity.

All of these benefits are relevant for children with Down's Syndrome.

A computer can offer access to a curriculum area in a non-judgemental way that allows the child to make mistakes and correct them without the disapproval of an adult. Through the use of appropriate computer software, areas of the curriculum that would appear particularly challenging can be made accessible and the child encouraged to participate. One danger of a high level of computer use is that children may become isolated from their peers. However, many programs are ideally suited to group work, through games or cooperative problem-solving. Children of differing levels of ability can work together to complete a task, each adopting a role that matches their individual profile of skills. Alternatively, programs can be selected for peer tutoring, with a more able child working with the child with Down's Syndrome.

Word-processing programs can not only help children record their ideas on paper, but also via the written word they can develop their vocabulary and grammatical knowledge. Many of the activities described in the sections on reading, writing, spelling and number can be carried out effectively on the computer, without the need for teachers to make complicated pieces of equipment. Children with Down's Syndrome can be given access to large quantities of information via computerised databases and the Internet. Data gathered by pupils can be stored and then organised by the computer to produce graphs or charts, without the need for the child to cope with the difficulties of drawing them with a ruler and pencil.

Painting or design programs can be used by the child with poor manipulative skills to create original posters, produce fabric designs or draw fancy borders around pieces of writing. Combined with a colour printer and the ability to enlarge, possibilities are endless. In the same way, students can use music programs to compose their own tunes, which the computer can then play back without the need for the child to handle an instrument. By working in this way, concentration and fine-motor skills can be enhanced.

In choosing software for the student with Down's Syndrome, Hawkridge and Vincent (1992) suggest that teachers ask the questions outlined in Figure 5.4. Since investing in computer systems and a range of appropriate software is an expensive exercise, it is important that schools seek advice and help from a local advisory service or a national resource centre such as Rickett Educational Media (REM – see appendix for address). With the right equipment, learning opportunities for students with Down's Syndrome can be increased immeasurably as well as making learning fun.

Developing abilities in physical education

'Children and adolescents with Down's Syndrome have a range of physical problems and difficulties that may affect their motor development. Therefore, it is important that programming which is directed towards facilitating motor skill development reflects quality practice' (Jobling, 1994).

As children with Down's Syndrome move up the school, continued attention needs to be paid to physical development to ensure that they are physically educated. Graham (1992) defines this as demonstrating the following.

- They have learned skills necessary to perform a variety of physical activities.
- They are physically fit.
- They participate regularly in physical activity.
- They know the implications and benefits of involvement in physical activity.
- They value physical activity and its contributions to a healthy lifestyle.

1. Does the software empower the user? Does it enable the user to do something they wanted to do but couldn't do without the computer?

2. Does the software give the student access to the National Curriculum or address the targets in their Individual Education Plan?

3. Is the software adaptable? Can it be used, with suitable modification, by a range of students with different needs?

4. Does the software offer cues and appropriate rewards? Is the student given regular feedback on their performance?

5. Is the program easy to use? Can it be used without continual adult help?

6. Is the text, on screen and in print, large and clear enough? Does it use colour and graphics to make it interesting and keep the student's attention?

Figure 5.4 Choosing computer software

Jobling (1994) suggests that students with Down's Syndrome have particular difficulty with timing, with balance and with the coordination of movements. Thus the development of these skills needs to be encouraged. Physical education programmes also need to focus on body and spatial awareness. The general fitness level of students with Down's Syndrome tends to be low. To some extent this may be attributable to physiological factors or heart problems.

However, there is also a lack of expectation from parents and teachers and hence a tendency for children and adolescents with Down's Syndrome to become obese, aggravating the problem further. Suggestions for activities that can be introduced into the primary PE curriculum can be found in a useful book by Pointer (1993), while ideas for older students can be found in a chapter by Reid and Black (1996) in *New Approaches to Down's Syndrome* edited by Stratford and Gunn.

In addition to improving their physical skills, it is important that young people with Down's Syndrome develop an understanding of the concepts within games, such as winning, losing and doing your best. Where the gap between the skills of students with Down's Syndrome and their peers is so great as to prevent the practice of key skills without interfering with the enjoyment of the other pupils, alternative strategies need to be considered. While it is possible for students to work individually with a teacher or support assistant, it might be more appropriate for them to adopt the role of 'assistant teacher' and spend time 'helping' a younger age group with an equivalent level of skill. Alternatively, they can work cooperatively with other students who dislike games or find them difficult because of physical disabilities, poor health or obesity.

A range of opportunities for movement should be introduced, including team games, dance, gymnastics, cycling, walking and swimming, both as part of the school curriculum and as a lunchtime or after-school activity. These should be chosen to fit in with the lifestyle of the family and designed to maximise the chance that they will be maintained once the student leaves school. Certainly as individual case histories indicate, young people with Down's Syndrome have considerable joint flexibility and can become highly proficient athletes, gymnasts and swimmers if encouraged in the early years. For those readers wishing to extend their knowledge in this area, *Down's Syndrome – Moving Through Life* by Burns and Gunn (1993) is a particularly useful book, covering all aspects of physical development.

Chapter 6

Developing Literacy and Numeracy Skills

Much of the material in this section has been derived from *Teaching Reading to Children with Down's Syndrome* by Patricia Olwein, published by Woodbine Press, and from *Meeting the Educational Needs of Children with Down's Syndrome* by Gillian Bird and Sue Buckley published by the University of Portsmouth.

Speaking and listening

Once the child with Down's Syndrome has acquired a basic spoken vocabulary, materials such as *The Derbyshire Language Scheme* (Knowles and Masidlover, 1982) are particularly useful in extending both expressive and receptive skills. Schools wishing to use this programme should look to their local speech and language therapy service or to their educational psychologist, to provide training for teachers and support assistants. Useful ideas can also be found in two books by Bill Gillham (1979 and 1983). Despite being rather dated in their presentation, they still contain lots of useful suggestions for the development of structured language programmes.

As the child's language skills develop, attention will need to be paid to syntax (the way in which language is structured) and to semantics (the meaning conveyed by the spoken word). Both areas present problems for most young people with Down's Syndrome, who appear to have more difficulty than other children at a similar level of cognitive development. While people with Down's Syndrome are likely to continue to extend their vocabulary throughout life, they tend to restrict themselves to more concrete words, particularly nouns, because of difficulties in abstract thinking.

Nevertheless, in everyday life this should not present any major obstacle to communication. In relative terms, children with Down's Syndrome appear to be particularly competent with the pragmatics (or social uses) of language. With practice and encouragement, most children with Down's Syndrome learn the unwritten rules of conversation and how to adapt their language to the demands of different situations. As they get older, however, they often fall behind their peers and need help in asking questions, seeking clarification or keeping to the topic in hand. The development of these skills, according to Bray (1995), will help the young person with Down's Syndrome overcome some of the problems of dysfluency or stammering commonly found. Further, by modifying their own behaviour (see Figure 6.1), others can help the young person communicate more effectively.

Teaching children to read

The realisation that reading with meaning was an attainable goal for children with Down's Syndrome has been a highly significant development of the last two decades. We now accept that they can learn to recognise words from as early as two or three years of age. Further, teaching children with Down's Syndrome to read is probably the most effective way of improving both their language and their ability to think and reason.

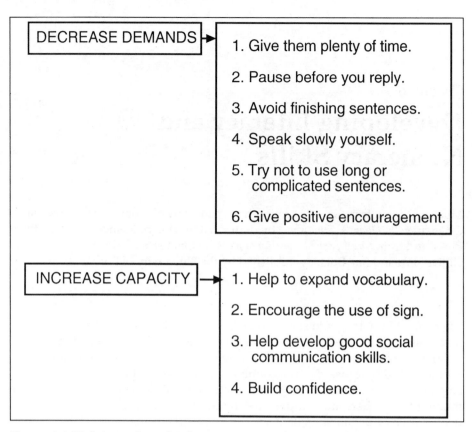

Figure 6.1 Helping reduce dysfluency

The processes involved, although similar to those occurring in normally developing children, differ in several distinct ways. For the majority of ordinary children, the development of speech and language comes well before they are introduced to reading. Thus, when they start to read, they already have a large vocabulary of words they can say and understand. They also know how words are combined to make sentences and the rules which govern the way sentences are put together. When faced with an unfamiliar word in a book, they are often able to guess what it says from its place in the sentence or from the context.

Young children with Down's Syndrome have neither a large vocabulary nor a knowledge of language structures to help them in learning to read. Nevertheless, they do seem able to recognise whole words by sight and by so doing, expand both their spoken vocabulary and their knowledge of grammar. Each time they are presented with a new word, they have to learn to recognise it in print and in speech, to say it and to understand it. Yet, they seem capable of doing this very effectively from an early age.

There is no reason why children with Down's Syndrome cannot be introduced to reading at the same age as other children. Not all will succeed, although there seem to be no reliable ways of determining reading readiness. However, the method used is of utmost importance. While children with good language skills can be introduced to reading through phonics, this approach does not work as well for children with Down's Syndrome. Since they lack both a sound base of language knowledge and have difficulties in processing auditory information, phonic approaches present major problems.

Key words are introduced initially on flash cards, using a clear consistent script. The first words that children learn should be those most familiar to them – e.g. their own name and the names of family members. These can be followed by words that describe objects from their direct experience – e.g. dog, car, house, school, teacher, book. The initial tasks for children to carry out (see Figure 6.2a) are:

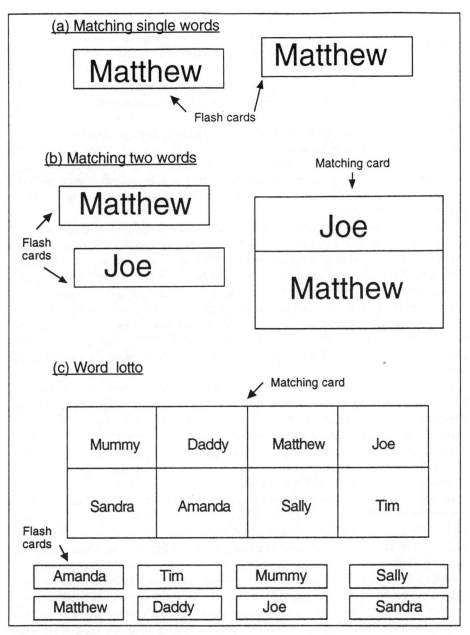

Figure 6.2 Teaching word matching skills

- to match the word on the flash card to an identical word
- to repeat the word aloud after the teacher
- to indicate in some way – e.g. pointing to themselves or a photo – that they understand what the word means.

Once the child understands about matching, a second word can be introduced and the child asked to select the correct match (see Figure 6.2b). Ideally the words should look quite different, to avoid visual confusion. Eventually the child can be playing a form of lotto, matching up to eight or ten words at a time (see Figure 6.2c). Initially, this work is best done individually, to allow the teacher or support assistant to give the child as much help as is needed to ensure success. Once the child is confident with the task, other children can be introduced and further work carried out in a group. Useful materials to reinforce these activities can be obtained from the Down Syndrome Educational Trust (DownsEd) at the Sarah Duffen Centre in Portsmouth (see Appendix 2 for address).

It is important for the teacher, or support assistant working with the child, to distinguish between testing and teaching. A child who is continually asked questions to which there is only one correct answer is likely to develop a range of diversionary tactics to avoid failure. To increase motivation, learning needs to be fun and to result in success. It is not cheating when the child looks at the picture on the flash card before telling the teacher what it says, just a step in the learning process.

Knowing that help is there will encourage children to take risks until, eventually, they can complete the task without it. Errorless learning techniques, such as moving the child's hand to the correct flash card (physical prompting), pointing to the correct card (gestural prompting) or using phrases such as: 'Are you sure?' or 'Have another think' (verbal prompting), are important tools in effective teaching.

Having learned how to match, the child can be taught to select words on request: 'Give me the word for . . .". Again, flash cards should be used and the child asked to repeat the word aloud. To encourage the development of understanding, pictures or photographs can be stuck to the back of the cards. These can be used by children to check that they have picked the correct card and will help them remember the meaning of the spoken word, if they are still not sure. This is a particularly good way of introducing new words into the child's vocabulary. Research has shown (Buckley, 1995), that children with Down's Syndrome are more likely to use words they have read, than words they have only heard.

Finally, the child should be encouraged to read words aloud. Where children are not yet speaking, but are competent users of a signing system, they can use the correct sign instead of saying the word. Having acquired a sight vocabulary, children can be introduced to books. Either they can be helped to make their own, combining familiar words and photographs to make a story about their lives or they can be taught words from the school's reading scheme and given access to the same books as their peers.

In all reading activities, attention must be paid to the development of comprehension skills as well as to reading accuracy. While it is clear that young children with Down's Syndrome do gain meaning from their early attempts at reading and are not just 'barking at print', there is a danger that their success at reading will encourage them to move on too fast, leaving their language development behind. As research has shown, maximum benefit from reading can only be gained if reading and language development progress together.

Once the child with Down's Syndrome has a basic sight vocabulary of around 50 words, then the early print to sound rules can be introduced. Without phonic skills, children's reading progress is likely to slow down or even come to a stop. Not only will they have no more room in their visual memory for new words, but also they will have no strategies for tackling words that they have not already learned. However, because of the difficulties they experience in processing and storing auditory information, the development of phonic skills is likely to be quite slow. As a direct consequence, many able children with Down's Syndrome will appear to reach a plateau in reading at around the level of an average eight-year-old.

Nevertheless, with structured input, progress can be made using an approach that stresses the similarities between words the child is already able to read. Modern approaches suggest that children should be taught about onsets, the sounds at the beginnings of words (e.g. 'fl' in 'flag', 'str' in 'string' and 'sh' in 'ship') and about rimes, the final sounds (e.g 'ag' in 'flag', 'ing' in 'string' and 'ip' in 'ship') rather than the sounds made by individual letters. Once the basic idea of sounding out words has been established, a comprehensive phonic programme such as THRASS (Davies and Richie, 1997) is worth considering, although the language used may require simplification.

At each stage in the development of reading, the teacher needs to move the child from the acquisition of new skills, to fluency in performing them. This is best done by giving children regular opportunities to practise skills they have already mastered (overlearning). Practice will also help them store the new learning more effectively in their long-term memory. At the same time as developing fluency in reading, it is important that children are taught to transfer their newly acquired skills from one set of teaching materials to another. A word read successfully from a white card with green printing, must also be recognised when handwritten in black. To aid this process, the child should be introduced to familiar words written in different ways, in different sizes and colours.

Finally, children should be taught to generalise their skills to a wide range of practical situations. Words or sentences recognised on flash cards should be equally meaningful when printed in the child's reading book, written on the side of a cereal packet or displayed on the television screen at the start of a programme. A variety of activities can be used to aid generalisation.

- Names can be attached to bottles of milk for the child to give out.
- Simple instructions can be written on the board or the computer.
- Lists of equipment for a task can be given to the child for them to assemble.

Where written instructions are to be used with the older child – e.g. on worksheets – it may be more effective to teach any unfamiliar words on flash cards first, before presenting the worksheet, rather than going over the instructions afterwards when the child has already experienced failure. Finally, it is important that children with Down's Syndrome are taught to recognise cursive script. Without this skill they will never be able to read letters or handwritten messages and will find it harder to develop joined writing of their own.

Developing writing skills

While the majority of young children with Down's Syndrome find the acquisition of reading relatively easy, writing almost invariably presents them with difficulties. Children starting in the Reception class, may not yet be ready for formal writing. However, they should be encouraged to experiment and become comfortable with a wide range of drawing and writing materials. Try to make all activities fun and meaningful. Drawing the stripes on a zebra is more interesting than copying straight lines. Tracing circles or stars for the Christmas decorations means more than merely tracing shapes on a work card.

Writing as a distinct task should be introduced when the child shows an interest and wants to have a try. This is often the case in a mainstream school where all the other children are writing. Let children 'write' their names at the top of their work like all their peers. Even though the product is merely a scribble at first, it helps establish the purpose of writing. In developing letter formation, different approaches should be tried, to see which works best for the individual. Some children are happy to cooperate with a structured series of activities, progressing from overwriting and tracing to free writing. Others prefer to experiment on their own, using unlined paper, for some time, before starting on a writing programme.

Once children can read their own names or those of other people they can start learning to write the same words. Visual aids to encourage correct pencil grip can be helpful in some cases – e.g. drawing a dog on the child's hand between the thumb and first finger, to be stroked by the child's pencil during writing (see Figure 6.3). Triangular pencils may be easier for the child to manipulate and felt tips may flow more easily than pencils. Some children are helped by pencil grips, such as Learning Development Aids' (LDA's) 'Tri-Go' (see Appendix 2 for address), or by an elastic band wound round the pencil to indicate where it

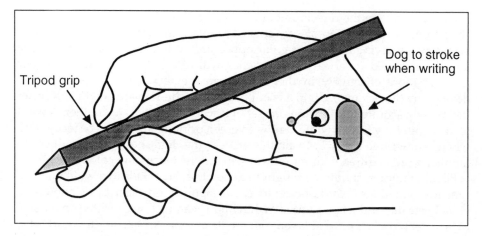

Tripod grip

Dog to stroke
when writing

Figure 6.3 Correct pencil grip

should be held. If children are reluctant to use a pencil or pen, other multisensory techniques, such as drawing letter shapes in sand or in shaving foam squirted onto a tray, can be a more acceptable way into writing. In most instances, the following sequence of activities is recommended.

1. Present the child with a familiar word, written clearly on a piece of paper or card. Ask the child to write over it with a brightly coloured felt-tip pen or crayon. Motivation can be increased by using games such as 'covering up the letters to keep them warm'.
2. Let the child trace words and then use them in the classroom. Names can be cut out, stuck on to card and used to label work trays or bottles of milk. Other words can be stuck under pictures as part of a wall display.
3. Produce dot-to-dot versions of words for the child to complete. Gradually increase the space between the dots.
4. Encourage the child to underwrite words from a model written clearly on the same piece of paper. Keep it large and use a consistent script, preferably with flicks to the letters, to make joined-up writing easier at a later stage. Combine words the child can read to make simple sentences.
5. Let the child copy words from a model written on a separate piece of card. Again try to make the words meaningful.
6. Encourage copying from a wall display or the board – e.g. the day, date and month at the top of a piece of work.
7. Dictate familiar words for the child to write from memory. Let the child tell you a story or a piece of news, write it down and then dictate it back one word at a time. This way a piece of writing can be built up over several sessions.

Because of their good visual skills, children with Down's Syndrome will benefit more from a large diagram of each letter with arrows or mice indicating the way their pencil should move (see Figure 6.4) than from verbal directions such as 'Down, up, round' on their own. However, these can still be used as backup. Commercially produced materials such as 'Rol 'n Write' letters from LDA can also be a help, as they provide a visual model for correct letter formation. Lined paper will help the child produce evenly sized and spaced letters. Olwein (1994) recommends the use of paper with coloured lines marking the top and bottom of letters, and draws a little man with his hat on the top line, his belt on the middle line and his feet on the bottom, as a visual aid.

Many children with Down's Syndrome are competent readers and are keen to make up their own stories before they can write words for themselves. In these instances, the provision of a word bank on small cards, which the child can use to build his or her own sentences, is recommended. These sentences can then be

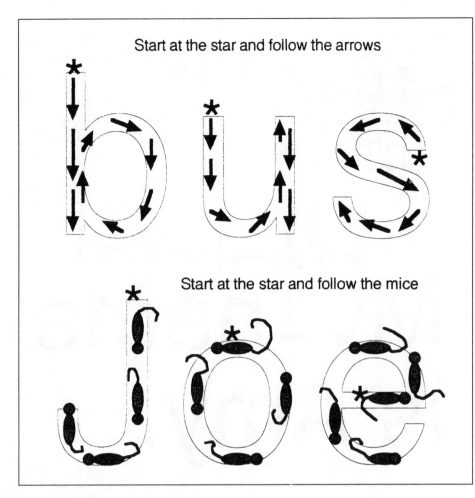

Start at the star and follow the arrows

Start at the star and follow the mice

Figure 6.4 Correct letter formation

written in the child's book by the support assistant or used as a model for the child to copy. Another method is to provide the child with a series of words written on stickers which can be selected and stuck into an exercise book without the need for adult help. To encourage the use of spaces between words, the child can be given a cardboard 'space man', who can sit on words with his legs in the space (see Figure 6.5).

Older children with Down's Syndrome should be taught to use a keyboard and given access to a word processor. This will enable them to get their ideas down on paper in a legible form, without the struggle of handwriting. Fine-motor difficulties can be overcome by the use of a concept keyboard, which allows the child to select whole words or sentences. Alternatively, the child can be taught to use a tape recorder or dictaphone and to dictate his or her own stories. These can then be transcribed by a support assistant, or even the school secretary, to provide a permanent record.

Teaching spelling

In the early years, children should be taught to write the words they can read by copying the whole word. Once they have developed a basic sight vocabulary, it is useful to help them break down words into their component letters and learn the rules of spelling. For this, it is important to have access to a range of materials including magnetic letters on a metal board, wooden letters or letters written on separate cards. Make sure that you have lower case as well as capital letters. The following sequence can be used as a guide (see Figure 6.6).

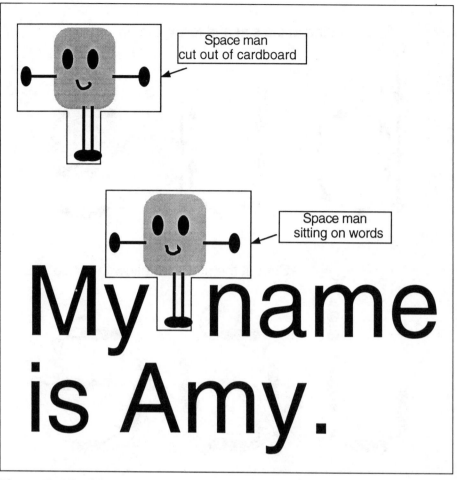

Figure 6.5 Word spacing

- Select the letters in a familiar word and encourage the child to match them onto a flash card of the whole word. Tell them the letter names as you work, but not the sound they make, as the same letter can sound very differently in different words (see Figure 6.6a).
- Encourage the child to arrange the individual letters in the correct order using the flash card as a model. Then turn over the flash card and remove one letter from the word. Give the child the letter to replace correctly saying its name. 'Where does the ___ go?' Let them refer back to the flash card to check (see Figure 6.6b).
- Remove two letters from the word and proceed in the same way.
- Mix up all the letters and help the child reassemble them in the correct order (see Figure 6.6c).
- Add some inappropriate letters to the pile and encourage the child to select those that are needed, before completing the word (see Figure 6.6d).

As they develop their skills, many children with Down's Syndrome will not need this practical apparatus. Instead they can be taught using the more usual 'Look, copy, cover, write, check' approach. For the child with Down's Syndrome, spelling should always be as visual a task as possible. However, there is also a place for the use of the tape recorder for spelling practice.

A tape that dictates words and then spells them out slowly, using letter names, can be useful in a busy classroom and provides an activity that the child can undertake without the need for adult supervision. The child, wearing headphones, can listen to the instructions and then write out the words. The completed work can then be taken to the teacher for marking. Computer

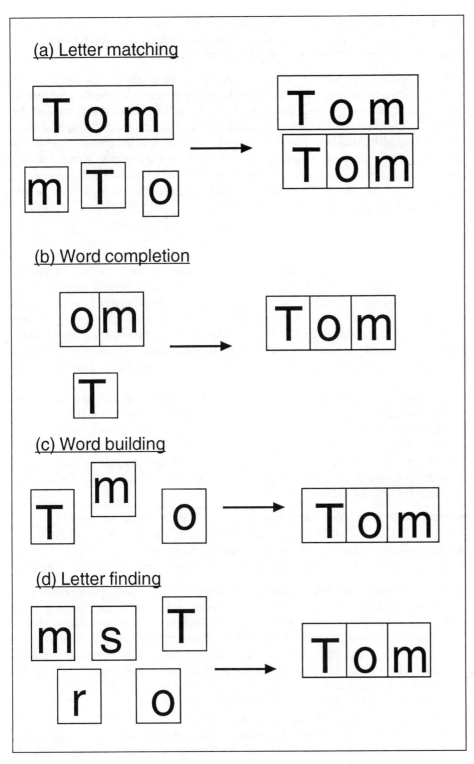

Figure 6.6 Developing spelling skills

programs are also available which operate in much the same way and can give feedback to the child as the program proceeds.

In the classroom, a range of cooperative games can be developed to aid spelling. These can include:

- Scrabble, using lower case letters
- simple crossword puzzles, using Scrabble letters or letters written on cards
- word searches

● paired spelling, with two children testing each other on their own words. (As long as the child with Down's Syndrome can read the other child's words, the two children can be working on quite different spelling lists.)

To aid spelling, picture dictionaries can be particularly useful for children with Down's Syndrome, once they have been taught how to use them. Normal dictionaries can prove very difficult, as they rely on the child's ability to hear the initial sounds in words. Once free writing has been established, children should be encouraged to build up their own word books or a word bank, using index cards in a box. Instead of using an alphabetic arrangement, words can be grouped under headings such as 'animals' or 'people'. Alternatively, they can be arranged alphabetically, but colour coded, with pictures representing the categories at the front of the book or the box.

Acquiring numeracy

Since the early 1970s, there has been considerable research on how normally developing children learn arithmetic. However, few investigations have involved children with Down's Syndrome. Given the dearth of research into how these children learn mathematical operations and concepts, it is not surprising that there is even less information on effective teaching approaches. Evidence currently available suggests that all students with Down's Syndrome experience significant difficulties in acquiring a working knowledge of mathematics.

Bird and Buckley (1994) suggest that typical children with Down's Syndrome spend the first years at school working towards Level 1 of the National Curriculum in maths. The most able are working towards, or have just achieved, Level 2 by the end of Key Stage 2, while some achieve Level 3 at secondary school. In a sample of 25 secondary-aged students, placed in mainstream schools, very similar results were obtained by the author, using the number checklist from Sloper *et al.* (1990):

● 2 were able to add and subtract numbers to 20 in their heads (Level 3)
● 6 were able to add and subtract numbers to 10 in their heads (Level 2)
● 13 were able to add and subtract, but still relied on concrete apparatus (Level 1)
● 4 could count, but could not yet add and subtract (working towards Level 1).

Despite the delay in skill acquisition, students with Down's Syndrome appear to develop mathematical concepts in the same way, and following the same stages, as their normally developing peers (Caycho, Gunn and Siegal, 1991). Difficulties that occur appear to be due to many of the same factors as those affecting other areas of learning. The development of mathematical thinking relies heavily on the understanding of a whole new language. Much of this language is abstract and difficult to represent visually. For children who find language learning a challenge, and the acquisition of abstract concepts difficult, mathematical thinking is bound to present problems.

While concrete apparatus is used extensively in the early years, the instructions that accompany tasks are almost invariably given verbally. Although the child appears to understand the task and can carry it out successfully under adult supervision, performance tends to fall off once the adult moves away. In many instances, this is not because children don't understand what they have to do or because they are unable to complete the task without help, but because they have forgotten the instructions. Here, yet again, the child's performance is restricted by a poor auditory memory.

Since children with Down's Syndrome tend to find it difficult to understand abstract processes, they may learn the routine involved in carrying out an operation without understanding its purpose. As a consequence, they may have real difficulty in applying their skills in new situations. A child who learns to count aloud by rote, without understanding that each counting word needs to be attached to an object, is likely to go on counting after the array of objects runs out. Similarly, children who learn to carry numbers, without understanding place value, can go very badly wrong when adding large numbers, without realising their mistake. To overcome some of these difficulties, the following approaches are recommended. They will not make maths easy, but they should help break down some of the barriers to success experienced by many children with Down's Syndrome.

1. Appropriate language should be taught, before it is used to carry out mathematical processes. LDA's Talking Maths photographs can be useful here, as can the pictures in many early maths books. Where children are able to read, key words should be written on flash cards and introduced into the child's reading vocabulary. Many children with Down's Syndrome have reading skills in advance of those found in normally developing children at similar levels of mathematical understanding. Wherever possible, these should be used to aid the acquisition of mathematical language.

2. All instructions and explanations should be accompanied by a visual reminder such as:
   - a similar task completed successfully – e.g. three hats already coloured in
   - visual prompt – e.g. a plastic 3 on the table, indicating three pictures to be coloured
   - a written instruction on a card – e.g.'Colour three frogs'.

3. Separate components of a task should be taught individually before they are combined (see Figure 6.7).

4. Mathematical progress should be assured by the use of a detailed small steps programme. A useful resource is the Mathsteps assessment and teaching programme from LDA, which covers: classifying, number, sequencing, spatial concepts, time, money, fractions, charts and volume, in a finely graded progression. Other useful ideas can be found in Bird and Buckley (1994) and in the Macquarie programme from Australia (Pieterse and Treloar, 1981).

5. Concrete and visual materials should be used wherever possible. When counting out sets of objects, children become less confused when given a container in which to place objects already counted. To aid number recognition, a number display, such as the Oxford Reading Tree Maths Frieze published by Oxford University Press, can be useful, while number lines, such as those available from AMS Educational, can be used to practise 'counting on' or 'counting back'. Wooden or plastic numbers can be particularly valuable in the primary classroom as can the 'Sum-Thing' bead abacus, from St. Joseph's Workshops or available through AMS. (See Appendix 2 for address of companies mentioned above).

Anecdotal evidence suggests that a high proportion of children with Down's Syndrome are unable to carry out even the simplest computations without using their fingers, a calculator or concrete apparatus such as counters or multilink cubes. The Touch Math approach, described by Hanrahan and Newman (1996), uses numerals with dots which the children touch as they count (see Figure 6.8). This method allows students at the single digit level of understanding to count on or back using only a pencil and paper.

This multisensory approach, in which the child counts aloud, looks at the numeral and touches the dots with the point of a pencil, is particularly suited to students with Down's Syndrome as it capitalises on their visual strengths. Initially, the child needs to be taught the touching sequence, with single dots for numerals 1–5 and double dots for numbers 6–9. In the initial stages, the

Task to be taught: 9-3 =

Subtasks

1. What do the digits 9 and 3 represent?

Make sure the child can identify the numerals 1–9, using number cards or plastic numerals.

2. How many objects are represented by the numerals 3 and 9?

Check that the child can select different numbers of blocks or counters from a larger selection.

3. What does 'taking away' mean and how does it differ from adding?

Practice adding blocks or sweets to a selection and then taking some away, using appropriate language.

4. What procedure should be used for taking away?

Teach the young child to select an agreed number of objects from a selection, take an agreed number away and then count those remaining. Rehearse the instructions – e.g. 'Find 9 bricks: 1, 2, 3, 4, 5, 6, 7, 8, 9, (**9 bricks here**). Take three away: 1, 2, 3, (**3 bricks gone**). Count those left:1, 2, 3, 4, 5, 6 (**6 bricks left**).' Older children can be taught to count backwards using a number line or Touch Math numerals (See Figure 6.8), again rehearsing the instructions as they work 'Start with 9 (**9**),take three away: 8, 7, 6 (**6 left**).'

5.What does the minus sign mean?

Teach addition and subtraction sums separately, then offer mixed selections and teach the child to recognise the appropriate signs.

6. What does the equals symbol mean?

Give the child practice in completing simple sums using +, − and = signs on cards with plastic or card numerals.

7. How should the answer be recorded?

Teach the child to write numerals or select appropriate stickers from a strip of stickers with numerals already written on them. Provide a written version of the sum with a space for the answer.

Figure 6.7 Teaching subtraction

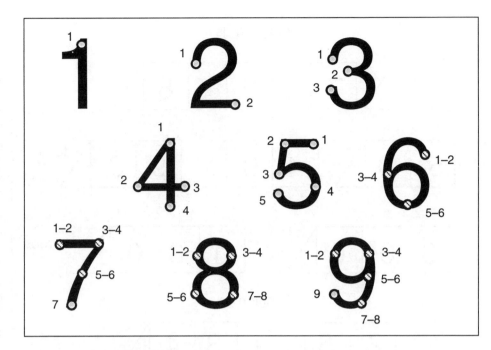

Figure 6.8 Touch Math numerals

dots should be marked on, using different colours for single and double dots. However, once the student has learned the correct procedure, markings on the digits can be dispensed with.

For those who have progressed beyond the single digit stage, Thompson (1997) describes a visual approach to place value. Hundreds, tens and units are represented by arrow cards, which are stacked to build larger numbers. In carrying out additions or subtractions, the child unpacks the number and then adds or subtracts the separate elements (see Figure 6.9). Students who are still uncertain about basic number bonds can use these materials in conjunction with counters, multilink cubes or a calculator.

6. Instructions, both verbal and written, should be kept short and simple. Worksheets should be simplified so that the child is faced with only one instruction at a time. Instructions are better written on a separate card, rather than on the sheet itself, to reduce distraction. Instructions should be rehearsed several times before the child is asked to complete the task. The task should then be carried out under adult supervision and the instructions rehearsed again, before the adult leaves the child to repeat the task several more times unaided, while repeating the instructions sub-vocally.

7. Opportunities should be offered to the child to generalise newly acquired mathematical skills. As with reading, children with Down's Syndrome may find it difficult to recognise a familiar mathematical task when presented in a different setting or using different materials. Newly acquired skills will need to be practised regularly, to ensure that they are consolidated, and applied in a range of situations. One-to-one correspondence can be practised by giving out milk bottles or hymn books. Sweets can be shared at break or an apple cut in half.

8. Confidence in understanding and using mathematical concepts needs to be built slowly and steadily. Although most children with Down's Syndrome learn to see themselves as competent readers and are keen to engage in reading-related tasks, this is rarely the case with mathematics. Since most maths activities are perceived as difficult and unrewarding for both the child and the teacher, they are often a source of conflict and frustration. However, with careful planning, progress can be made and sessions made enjoyable for both parties.

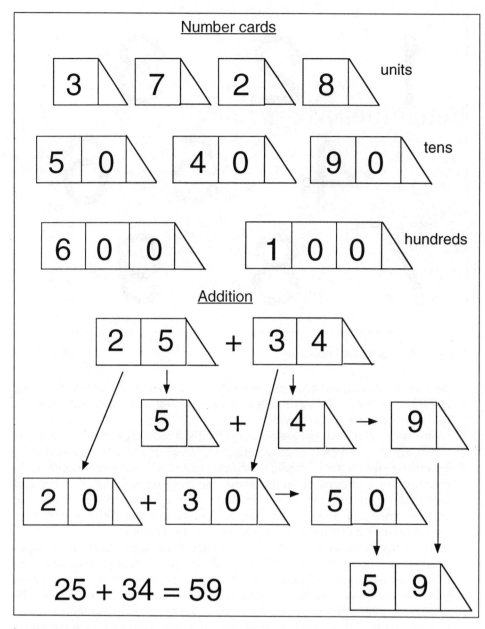

Figure 6.9 Place value

Chapter 7

Behaviour Management

Children with Down's Syndrome have typically been characterised as placid, affectionate, sociable and easy going, with good skills of imitation and a stubborn streak. This stereotype can be traced back to Langdon Down who described his 'mongolian idiots' in the following terms:

> They have considerable powers of imitation, even bordering on being mimics. They are humorous and a lively sense of the ridiculous often colours their mimicry . . . No amount of coercion will induce them to do that which they have made up their minds they will not do.

As those with experience of more than one child with Down's Syndrome will realise, there is considerable variability in the population. Nevertheless, some tendencies do appear to be common. Poor muscle tone and a slower-than-average response time render the young baby with Down's Syndrome rather less demanding than normally developing peers. Where parents are aware of the difficulties faced by their baby, and are proactive in stimulating and interacting with him or her, levels of activity and responsiveness will increase. If, on the other hand, the parent responds only to demands initiated by the child, the baby may become increasingly quiet and placid, without the desire to explore or develop new skills.

Even in older children, difficulties in communication can lead to them seeming less vocal than their peers and less willing to assert themselves. However, where adults and other children are willing to communicate using sign, or give children time to formulate their ideas, the young person with Down's Syndrome can be encouraged to participate in group activities. Increased confidence and self-esteem should lead in turn to higher levels of activity and involvement.

In general, social skills do appear to develop well. Most young people with Down's Syndrome, being more proficient in visual than in auditory processing, will be adept at the imitation of actions and will readily copy the behaviour of others. As Wishart (1996) has noted, competence in social interaction can also be used by children with Down's Syndrome as a device to avoid unwelcome demands. Where they are unable to divert attention away from the task in hand, many will simply refuse to comply or pretend to be less competent than they actually are.

Much of the behaviour observed in children with Down's Syndrome is related to their overall level of developmental delay. Not only will they show delays in physical and cognitive development, but their behaviour may also be immature. Learning more slowly than their peers, they will take longer to learn social rules such as taking turns, sharing or cooperating with others. It is important that immature behaviours are distinguished from those that are deliberately naughty or attention-seeking and that the child is helped gradually to behave in a more age-appropriate manner.

Numerous examples of this type of immaturity can be found in the literature. As O'Grady (1994), describing the integration of one young lady into a mainstream high school of 1,300 pupils, explains:

Personality and behaviour

61

Another early problem was Cherry's desire to show her affection for everyone by sometimes rushing up to teachers and peers to give them a hug. Those who had had little direct contact with her were a little taken aback and unsure as to how they should react, but they all learned and Cherry learned too! Slowly and without feeling rejected she has adopted more 'socially acceptable' forms of greeting and when to apply them. She is much more mature generally. For example she no longer hides under tables or closes her eyes and thinks no one can see her, nor does she leap out from behind corners to give us a surprise.

Causes of inappropriate behaviour

All young people can, at times, display behaviours which others consider to be inappropriate. This applies just as much to students with Down's Syndrome as it does to other young people. The reasons underlying such behaviours are also much the same. Inappropriate behaviours in school can be classified as those that:

1. cause harm to the child or to others
2. upset or annoy other people
3. interfere with the learning of the child or other school pupils
4. disrupt the smooth running of the organisation.

Most children display inappropriate behaviours for one or more of the reasons outlined in Figure 7.1.

All four conditions outlined in the figure apply, on occasions, to the behaviour of young people with Down's Syndrome. Before teachers are in a position to modify inappropriate behaviours, it is clearly essential that they understand their cause. Where children with Down's Syndrome have become used to having their own personal support assistant at their side for most of the day, they may have real difficulty in accepting the fact that he or she may begin to work with other children in the classroom. Attempts to increase independence in the child with Down's Syndrome, can result, initially, in displays of difficult, attention-seeking behaviour. Similarly, children who have been successful at avoiding work by smiling or changing the subject may well be thrown when faced by a teacher or assistant who realises that they are far more capable than they are making out and insist on the completion of the task. The result could be a tantrum, particularly if such behaviour has been successful in the past.

Students with Down's Syndrome keen to be the same as everyone else in the class can become angry and frustrated if the teacher insists on them doing their own special work while the rest of the class members are involved in a totally different activity. On the other hand, if allowed to take part without adequate thought having been given to differentiation, they may be faced with insuperable difficulties and, as a consequence, may become awkward or disruptive. Frustration can also occur when children are faced with people unwilling to listen or unable to understand what they are trying to say. If not resolved, this may lead to undesirable behaviour on the part of the child.

Schools, particularly in the secondary sector, are complex organisations with a large number of rules. All children take time to learn what is expected of them, particularly at times of transition. Not only are they faced with the task of understanding a whole series of rules, most of which are explained verbally and without a visual prompt, but also they are expected to retain this information over the long term. This can prove a formidable task for students with limited comprehension skills and a poor auditory memory. It is not surprising that students with Down's Syndrome often get confused and forget what they have been told.

This confusion can, at times, be used by other children as a source of amusement. Children with Down's Syndrome are only rarely subject to

1. Because they want adult attention.

- They know what they are doing is naughty.

- They have done it before and know it works.

- They would rather be punished than ignored.

2. Because they are angry or frustrated.

- Anger is building up and needs to be let out.

- They lash out at whoever is nearby.

- They need to regain some control over their lives.

3. Because they are uncertain or confused.

- They are unsure of what is expected.

- They don't realise that it is unacceptable.

- They have done it before without being told off.

4. Because it gives them pleasure.

- The rewards over ride the consequences.

- It helps them unwind or calm down.

- They don't notice that people are getting cross.

Figure 7.1 Why children misbehave

bullying. Nevertheless, they can be set up by others and encouraged to play the fool. This may be seen as an effective way of gaining attention. Alternatively, it may be that they do not realise that they are being asked to behave inappropriately and so become upset when told off. If situations in school have been handled badly and the child has become quite isolated and unhappy, self-stimulatory behaviour such as rocking, thumb-sucking or genital stimulation may occur. Where the child is well integrated and in receipt of an appropriate combination of challenge and support, such behaviours are rare in the school situation. However, where they do occur, they should be seen as a warning and particular attention paid to the way the child is being managed.

Preventing serious problems

Many of the difficulties outlined above can be avoided with a bit of thought and preparation in advance (see Figure 7.2). Cooperation between home and school is important, as is joint planning between teacher and support assistant. Other school staff, such as the secretary and lunchtime supervisors, also need to be involved as a consistent approach to management is essential. Well-meaning dinner ladies, who allow the child with Down's Syndrome to go to the front of the queue or give them extra pudding, can cause real problems. Similarly, an untrained support assistant who regularly allows the child to opt out of activities or who follows the child everywhere, will inhibit the development of age-appropriate behaviours.

School and class rules need to be taught simply and clearly from the beginning and the child reminded of them at regular intervals. Pictures of the main rules can be useful, or a written version provided once the child can read. All infringements should be noted and the child encouraged to realise which rule has been broken. Punishments are only appropriate where staff are quite sure that the child has deliberately broken a rule and is seeking attention. Nonetheless, children with Down's Syndrome need to be treated just as firmly as anyone else. Once the basic rules have been established, no exception should be made. Confrontations are best avoided, although the child's own avoidance tactics need to be identified and discouraged early on.

Work must be carefully planned and differentiated to ensure that the child achieves success. However, where possible, the child should remain in the classroom and be involved in class activities. Insisting that children with Down's Syndrome work on their handwriting or spelling when everyone else is doing drama or painting pictures, is insensitive and is likely to cause problems. These tasks are far better done when the others are also writing or learning spellings, even if the content of the work is different. Where special work is required, such as a structured language programme, this should be done when the class members are engaged in activities the child dislikes or is unable to access. Removing the child from the room for a short period of time for this special work is often more successful as there is less distraction from competing activities.

Unstructured times require thought, although it is important that, where possible, the child is allowed to socialise and play with normally developing peers without continual adult supervision. Withdrawal during times such as assembly should be avoided, as informal interactions are essential for the development of friendships and help the child become more independent. Although the safety of the child is clearly paramount, other children can prove sensible and reliable monitors – e.g. ensuring that the child with Down's Syndrome does not wander from the playground. Some schools use a rota of older children who gain credit for this particular responsibility. Others set up Circles of Friends who are active in ensuring that the child with Down's Syndrome is happy and well integrated into school life, without the risk of becoming overdependent on adults. Such peer-group support can also provide an effective check against teasing or bullying.

Sexual development and behaviour

According to Van Dylce *et al.* (1995), 'All individuals, regardless of disability are sexual beings. Individuals with Down syndrome and other mental disabilities who engage in sexual behaviours, however, may encounter social prejudice as well as significant parental anxiety'.

For students with Down's Syndrome attending mainstream schools, this anxiety almost invariably extends to their teachers who wish to ensure the safety of a vulnerable young person. Explaining the physical, and more particularly the psychological, aspects of sexuality to students whose physical development far outstrips their emotional development, is of particular concern.

1. Hold consistent expectations
(a) Ensure all teachers and non-teaching staff have appropriate and shared expectations of behaviour.
(b) Discourage special favours or allowances.
(c) Remind the student about school and class rules.
(d) Work closely with the parents to ensure they support school rules.

2. Provide clear instructions
(a) Ensure the student understands the rules.
(b) Check that the rules have been remembered.
(c) If necessary, use individual counselling sessions to discuss behaviour and ways of dealing with problems.
(d) Explain why the rules may be different in different settings.

3. Avoid frustration
(a) Give the student time to talk to a trusted adult.
(b) Encourage staff to discuss problems with each other to arrive at explanations and solutions.
(c) Encourage peers to be supportive and watch out for bullying.
(d) Ensure the student is only excluded from activities when absolutely necessary and that an explanation is offered.

4. Liaise with parents
(a) Keep parents informed, but do not report every hiccup.
(b) Devise behavioural strategies cooperatively.
(c) Draw on parental expertise in devising a programme.

Figure 7.2 Preventing behaviour problems

Physically, most young people with Down's Syndrome develop in just the same way as their peers. In boys, undescended testicles are rather more common than in the population as a whole, but rarely present a problem as effective treatment is readily available. Levels of male hormone appear to be somewhat depressed in young men with Down's Syndrome. In some individuals this causes a sparseness or even absence of facial and pubic hair, as well as the more usual reduction in sperm count. Nevertheless, adolescent boys with Down's Syndrome show typical teenage concerns. Masturbation is as common as in other boys of a similar age and should be treated in just the same way, as a healthy and normal part of self-discovery, but an activity that should be carried out in private.

Kingsley and Levitz (1994), two young men with Down's Syndrome, express clearly their interest in girls, sex and marriage and their worries about the etiquette of dating. Anecdotal evidence suggests that many boys in mainstream settings are keen to have a girlfriend. However, the chance of them finding a partner in an integrated setting will not be great and they may need opportunities to mix socially with girls of a similar level of maturity. Girls with Down's Syndrome generally start menstruating at much the same age as their peers. Although fertility is somewhat reduced, there is a risk of pregnancy and so issues of contraception need to be dealt with during sex education lessons.

Of even greater concern is the need to protect children with Down's Syndrome from exploitation or sexual abuse. Many are outgoing, affectionate and trusting, and so personal safety education should begin early in childhood. Young children may learn best from a good touch/bad touch model (Haka-Ikse and Mian 1993). Older students, on the other hand, may be able to learn the 'Circles concept' (Walker-Hirsch and Champagne 1992). Here, coloured circles represent levels of personal relationship and physical intimacy (see Figure 7.3).

The Purple Private Circle represents the individual concerned. The Blue Hug Circle comes next. This represents those people who are closest to the person in the purple circle, both physically and emotionally. Close family or partners are generally placed in this circle, where close body hugs are the norm. Next comes the Green Far Away Hug Circle. Close friends and extended family members tend to be assigned to this circle. The Yellow Handshake Circle, for friends and acquaintances whose names are known, comes next, then the Orange Wave Circle for other more distant acquaintances. No physical or emotional contact is involved at this level of intimacy. Finally there is the Red Stranger Space. No physical contact or conversation is exchanged with people in this circle, unless the person is identified by a recognisable badge or uniform.

Like all young people, students with Down's Syndrome need early sex education coupled with open discussion. They need to be made aware of sexually transmitted diseases and will require a lot of help in responding appropriately to members of the opposite sex without exposing themselves to rejection or ridicule. Opportunities to mix socially with both learning disabled and normally developing peers of both sexes should be offered during leisure time and a sympathetic adult, outside the immediate family, should be available to enable the young person to discuss sensitive or personal problems in confidence.

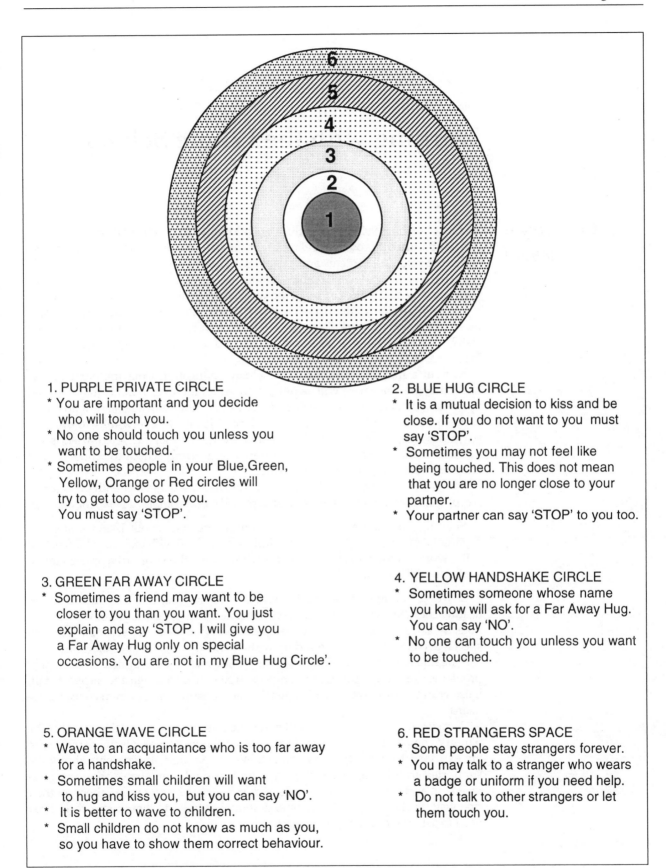

1. PURPLE PRIVATE CIRCLE
* You are important and you decide who will touch you.
* No one should touch you unless you want to be touched.
* Sometimes people in your Blue, Green, Yellow, Orange or Red circles will try to get too close to you. You must say 'STOP'.

2. BLUE HUG CIRCLE
* It is a mutual decision to kiss and be close. If you do not want to you must say 'STOP'.
* Sometimes you may not feel like being touched. This does not mean that you are no longer close to your partner.
* Your partner can say 'STOP' to you too.

3. GREEN FAR AWAY CIRCLE
* Sometimes a friend may want to be closer to you than you want. You just explain and say 'STOP. I will give you a Far Away Hug only on special occasions. You are not in my Blue Hug Circle'.

4. YELLOW HANDSHAKE CIRCLE
* Sometimes someone whose name you know will ask for a Far Away Hug. You can say 'NO'.
* No one can touch you unless you want to be touched.

5. ORANGE WAVE CIRCLE
* Wave to an acquaintance who is too far away for a handshake.
* Sometimes small children will want to hug and kiss you, but you can say 'NO'.
* It is better to wave to children.
* Small children do not know as much as you, so you have to show them correct behaviour.

6. RED STRANGERS SPACE
* Some people stay strangers forever.
* You may talk to a stranger who wears a badge or uniform if you need help.
* Do not talk to other strangers or let them touch you.

Figure 7.3 The Circles concept

Chapter 8

Working with the Whole School

Choosing a school

As Lincoln *et al.* (1992) note, 'Including children with severe learning difficulties in neighbourhood provision invariably means more work, more effort, more risk and more anxious moments and sleepless nights all round.'

In the North American model, schools are supported in including students with learning disabilities through the work of an Inclusion Facilitator. While this is a role unfamiliar to the British scene, it is useful to analyse the way in which these professionals work if we are to improve our practice. O'Brien and Forest (1989) describe the role in some detail and outline five essential steps to inclusion, as shown in Figure 8.1.

Without a major commitment to inclusive education from the parents, it is likely that the placement will be put at risk. At infant level, parents may be faced by schools that are clearly unwilling to take on a child with a label or who refuse to do so without full-time support, which the LEA may be unwilling to provide. At junior age, children may be rejected by the schools all their friends are moving to and parents may have to trail around from school to school to find another, more sympathetic, headteacher.

On transfer to secondary school, anxieties are increased together with pressures to accept special education. As one parent, reported by Lincoln *et al.* (1992), commented:

'Sending our children to the local comprehensive school is not a step we parents undertake lightly . . . I can fully sympathise with parents who feel that the worry involved is too great and who opt for the supportive environment of a special school.

However committed and skilled school staff may be, it is the attitude of the headteacher that is the key to successful inclusion. As Dyson and Millward (1997) note: 'It is our consistent finding that the response made by a particular school to special needs is intimately bound up with the head's view of special needs.'

A headteacher who understands the issues and is determined to overcome problems can set up appropriate systems in school, encourage and support staff, liaise with the LEA and outside agencies, and ensure that parental concerns are heard.

Occasionally, an LEA officer will make the initial approach to the school of the parents' choice. However, this is rare. In most circumstances it is the parents who are expected to make the first contact. Where possible, the parents should be supported in this important step by a professional who shares their vision of inclusion and can coach the parents and, if necessary, accompany them on their first visit. In choosing a school, parents should always do their homework. They need to ask the following six questions.

Where do most children in the local area go to school?

Children with Down's Syndrome will benefit most when they attend the same school as children from their immediate neighbourhood. By so doing, they

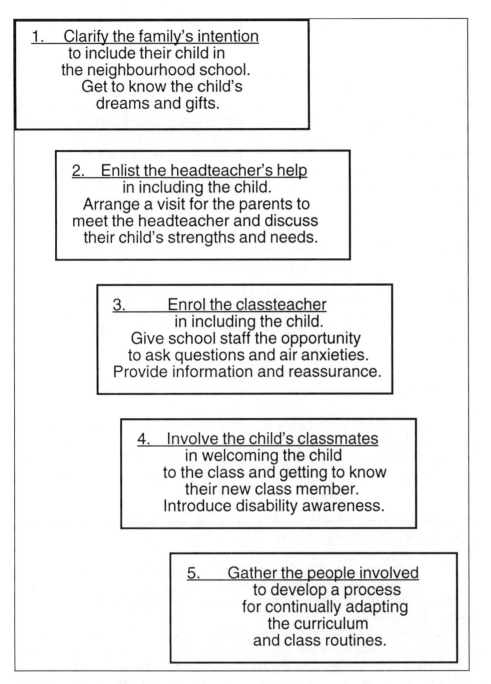

1. **Clarify the family's intention**
   to include their child in
   the neighbourhood school.
   Get to know the child's
   dreams and gifts.

2. **Enlist the headteacher's help**
   in including the child.
   Arrange a visit for the parents to
   meet the headteacher and discuss
   their child's strengths and needs.

3. **Enrol the classteacher**
   in including the child.
   Give school staff the opportunity
   to ask questions and air anxieties.
   Provide information and reassurance.

4. **Involve the child's classmates**
   in welcoming the child
   to the class and getting to know
   their new class member.
   Introduce disability awareness.

5. **Gather the people involved**
   to develop a process
   for continually adapting
   the curriculum
   and class routines.

Figure 8.1 Five steps to inclusion

maximise their chances of making local friends whom they can play with after school or in the holidays.

How is the school organised?

Reports from parents suggest that children with Down's Syndrome who have to change schools at 7 and 11, or at 9 and 13, generally have more problems in gaining acceptance than those attending one primary and one secondary school. Each transition presents a further hurdle for the child and the parents to overcome as each new adult they encounter needs time to see the child behind the label.

What support is generally offered to pupils with special educational needs?

Schools with an experienced Special Needs Coordinator (SENCO), who has an allowance of time to do her job, will find it easier to cater for a child with Down's Syndrome. Where the SENCO is a full-time class teacher, and no other support is provided for pupils with special needs, staff may feel overburdened and may be reluctant to take on what is seen as 'extra work'. Survey data indicate that most parents of children with Down's Syndrome discuss their child's progress with school staff on a regular basis. However, while secondary SENCOs are involved in 71 per cent of these meetings, primary SENCOs attend on less than 13 per cent of occasions.

Which local schools have taken children with Down's Syndrome in the past and how have those children got on?

Previous success in educating a child with Down's Syndrome is likely to have a positive influence on the attitude of the school to inclusion. Conversely, a placement that has 'failed' may make the school reluctant to try again.

What is the attitude of the LEA to inclusion and what package of support is likely to be offered?

Where LEAs have little experience of inclusion, parents may need the help of the local Parent Partnership Officer or a voluntary agency in negotiating with officers or, ultimately, in appealing to the SEN Tribunal. Alternatively, they may need to enlist the support of the school in seeking an adequate level of resourcing

What are the local school's priorities and how are children with learning difficulties likely to be received?

A school with a high rate of exclusion or one that sees itself as competing with its neighbours to secure more pupils, or achieve a high ranking in league tables, may be less sympathetic than one that values all children and works closely with the local community.

At the first visit, the parents need to be clear about what they want – e.g. a full-time place with other children of the same age. They should describe the child positively and be honest about the type of extra help likely to be required and the times when coping without support is possible. They need to explain why gaining a place at that school is of importance to the family and should stress the benefits of inclusion for the child. Finally, the parents should offer to bring the child for a visit when the head has had time to talk to staff and to governors.

Involving the staff

Once the school has agreed to admit the child, contact should be made with the chosen class teacher to explore anxieties before the child starts. As O'Brien and Forest (1989) note:

> Many of the good teachers we have met don't see themselves as able to teach children with special needs . . . Though they may not believe it until they have experienced inclusion for themselves, inclusion draws on the same capacities that make them good teachers of any child' (*see* Figure 8.4).

ALL GOOD TEACHERS:

* respond to individual differences among students by adapting curriculum and routines

* involve all students in class work by using a variety of instructional methods

* create a safe environment that encourages responsible, cooperative behaviour

* collaborate and share teaching tasks effectively with teaching assistants

* make good use of advisory staff without giving up responsibility for their class

* build networks with colleagues to renew their sense of purpose and provide mutual help in problem-solving

* increase their own repertoire of skills and abilities.

Figure 8.2 The essence of a good teacher

To start the relationship between teacher and child as positively as possible, it is important that the teacher meets the child and talks to the parents, rather than reading too many formal reports that tend to stress what the child cannot do. Home visits or observations of the child in a playgroup or nursery can be helpful for the primary teacher, while secondary staff can usefully visit the child at primary school. Discussions with those who know the child well will often highlight strengths and dispel stereotypes, reassuring staff who may be apprehensive. Networking with staff at schools where placements are succeeding can be of particular benefit.

A meeting between the class teacher, the head, the SENCO and the parents, together with an outside facilitator, can be useful to identify the support that will be required and ways in which the timetable and classroom routines will need modifying. Ideally, the classteacher and parents should be involved in interviewing the support assistant who will be working with the child. Where this is not possible, meetings between parents and key staff should be arranged before the child starts.

Some support assistants who live locally are happy to visit the family over the summer holiday before the child starts the new school. Others will spend some time getting to know the child in the previous setting. Some schools, keen to build good working relationships between support assistants and teachers, will appoint the assistant before the child starts, allowing him or her time to get to know the school. All these strategies are valuable in building confidence.

Where a number of staff will be involved with the child, a group discussion led by an educational psychologist or advisory teacher can help iron out any worries and create a positive climate. Even where only one teacher will be involved initially, a presentation to the whole staff can be really useful. Governors and non-teaching staff, including welfare assistants and lunchtime supervisors should also be invited, as their commitment to the successful inclusion of the child is equally important.

By involving the whole school community from the beginning, there should be fewer problems in dealing effectively with any adverse comments from other parents, worried that their own child's education may suffer. Introductory videos such as *Education – Preparation for Life* produced by the Down's Syndrome Association and *Educational Choices for Children with Down's Syndrome*, available from Devon Learning Resources (see Appendix 2 for address), can be a useful stimulus for discussion.

Lincoln *et al.* (1992) suggest that anxiety levels for schools seem to peak towards the second half of the first term. By then, staff can see all the problems and none of the solutions. The fullest support from parents and external agencies is required at this stage to avoid hasty conclusions about the inappropriateness of the placement being drawn. However, even when initial anxieties have been overcome, there are bound to be difficulties which are best addressed collaboratively. Regularly programmed meetings of interested staff on a half termly basis, can be an effective way of nipping problems in the bud and providing a network of support for the class teacher.

Working with ordinary pupils

Practitioners in the field of inclusion hold mixed views about the appropriateness of discussing the special needs of the child with Down's Syndrome with other students. Some feel that such interventions, particularly with young children, highlight differences which might otherwise be accepted merely as a reflection of life's diversity. Others feel that alerting the class to the issues of inclusive education and the need to make children who are different feel welcome is of real importance.

In 1989, John Smeaton High School in Leeds, in planning for the inclusion of up to 12 students with severe learning difficulties, carried out an extensive awareness-raising programme with all its students. Pupils in the classes in which the new students would be placed were given background information by Paul Sibbons, June Wilson and their colleagues (personal communication). The discussions covered severe learning difficulties in general as well as some of the more specific problems individual students might present. Their peers were given a rationale for inclusion and asked for their support. All questions were answered honestly and no attempt was made to minimise the possible difficulties. Nevertheless, the emphasis remained positive throughout and pupils were encouraged to look forward to sharing classes with the new pupils.

Once the students with learning difficulties had been attending the school for nearly a year, a questionnaire was circulated to all the students in their forms (see Figure 8.3), asking for feedback. The returns were discussed, while the students concerned were out of the room, and solutions to identified problems put forward. Three years later, the same questionnaire was used again, to reinforce for the students the need for their ongoing commitment to inclusion. It also served to identify any changes in student attitudes over time. The success of the project can be gauged by some of the comments made by pupils of the school on the audio-tape *Talking Inclusion* (CSIE, 1994). Student views were obtained by an independent researcher shortly before the second questionnaire was administered. When asked whether peers with learning disabilities should be in the ordinary school or placed in special schools, their responses were quite clear:

- 'It's good having them because we can learn more having them with us'
- 'They're doing all right here. They've got friends here'.

The pilot project of integrating severe learning difficulty children into mainstream school is reaching the end of the year. Your help was sought last September when the project began, and therefore it is only proper that you also are given the opportunity to comment. Please be as honest as you like but informative as well. Your sheet will be anonymous.

Initial reaction to the pupils in the class.

Present reaction to the pupils in the class.

How do you feel they cope with lessons in your class?

Do they get enough support?

How do they cope at break and lunchtime?

Do you think they should be in a normal school? State your reasons.

Do you feel you understand more about mental handicap now?

Do you feel the pupils have become part of the school?

Comments (anything else you wish to say about the pupils).

Thank you for your help this year.

Figure 8.3 Student questionnaire: 1990

- 'They'd be much better off in proper school, like our school, because there are people around to help them'.
- 'If they're going [to special school] we're going. It just wouldn't be right'.

Most schools with an inclusive philosophy offer some form of disability-awareness training which encompasses the whole range of special needs. At primary level, *Lessons for Inclusion* (Vandercook *et al.*, 1994) offers a range of ideas on including everyone, self-esteem, making and keeping friends, and cooperation. Two excellent resources for older students are *Disability Equality in the Classroom* (Rieser and Mason, 1992) and *Altogether Better* (Mason and Rieser, 1994).

All staff need to agree how they will respond to questions from other students about a pupil with Down's Syndrome. While there are relatively few books for children about disability in general or Down's Syndrome in particular, *Our Brother has Down's Syndrome* (Cairo, 1985), *Nothing Special* (Mason, 1989) and *It's Good To be Different* (Milicic, 1994) are among the best currently available for younger pupils. For older children *My Brother, Matthew* (Thompson, 1992) and *Thumbs Up, Rico* (Testa, 1994) are useful, although clearly designed for the North American market. Schools should also look out for a new book *Thinking About Having a Learning Disability* (Flynn and Flynn, 1998) to be published in London later this year.

Circles of friends

As Wilson and Newton (1996) point out:

> Each of us needs friends and fears isolation from others. Our psychological well-being is tied up in our relationships and closeness to other people. Within these relationships we discover who we are and who we can be. Without such relationships we lose our bearings. We can behave in ways we do not understand because there is no one to help us make sense of what we are feeling and how we are acting.

For children with Down's Syndrome, a mainstream school can be a very confusing place, beset with rules and routines very different from those they are familiar with at home. Other children may be wary of making an approach or including the child in their games or conversations, particularly if there is always an adult minder at hand. Children who are keen to offer practical support may be discouraged for fear that such involvement may 'exploit' them or interfere with their work.

Yet we know that children benefit greatly from helping each other. They develop tolerance, patience and understanding and, through teaching, extend their own skills. Children are undoubtedly far better than adults at assessing the climate and dynamics of school situations and frequently are more able to produce effective solutions to ongoing problems. By using this willing labour force, scarce resources can be concentrated where they are most needed. Yet the power of the peer group is used all too rarely to improve the experiences of children with Down's Syndrome in mainstream schools. As Foot *et al.* (1990) note:

> We are only just beginning to appreciate the richness of ways in which children might be capable of providing sources of practical assistance and emotional support as well as providing powerful influences upon each other's cognitive and social development.

Friendship occurs when two or more people discover common interests and develop a mutually satisfying relationship. On the other hand, peer support is the kind of help one student may give to another, sometimes via an adult's request. As Tashie *et al.* (1993) note, friends often provide peer support and peer supporters may become friends. Nevertheless, the two roles are quite separate and need to be distinguished, although both are important in creating inclusive classrooms.

One highly successful approach, being used increasingly to facilitate the development of both peer support and true friendships, is the Circle of Friends (Perske, 1988) first developed in North America. By using opportunities for discussion afforded by Circle Time (Curry and Bromfield, 1994) or Personal and Social Education (PSE), the class can be introduced to the idea. Through discussion, they can be helped to realise that all of us, particularly those who are unhappy or disadvantaged in some way, need friends. Individuals are encouraged to volunteer to be part of a circle of friends for the child with Down's Syndrome. The target child is then asked to select from those who volunteer or to ask others to take part.

The group meets with the target child and a member of staff on a weekly basis, to discuss ways in which the group can help the child to become more involved in school or class activities, reduce inappropriate behaviour or take part in events in the community. Once children with Down's Syndrome feel safe in the group they can be helped to articulate their own dreams and aspirations and share their worries. The group can focus on ways of showing the child that he or she is valued and can consider how to stop others from teasing or bullying them. The role of the teacher is to listen to the group's suggestions and find ways they can be achieved. Schools interested in pursuing the idea can find out more from the Circles Network in Bristol (see Appendix 2 for the address).

The basic circle of friends model (Pearpoint and Forest, 1992) consists of four concentric circles with the child in the middle (see Figure 8.4). The inner circle, or circle of intimacy, contains those people who are closest to the child, who love and are loved by them. The next circle, or circle of friendship, contains people who can be relied on for support and friendship. The third circle, or circle of participation, contains acquaintances and people who the child sees regularly but is not close to. Finally, the outer circle, or circle of exchange, contains people who are paid to be with the child, such as teachers, support assistants and speech therapists.

Initially, children with Down's Syndrome may have large numbers of people in their circle of exchange, but relatively few in their inner circles. The aim of the intervention is to fill in the inner circles and by so doing enrich the life of the child. Whatever form the circle takes, it is essential that the target child is at the centre and has a major say in who is included. At secondary level, a process used in New South Wales (Phillips, 1995) is recommended (see Figure 8.5) for building a student support team, which works in much the same way.

Peer tutoring

At its most basic level, peer tutoring involves children teaching other children, usually on a one-to-one basis. Tutors may be of the same age as the the child being tutored, or older. However, there is always a skill gap between the students involved. Peer tutoring differs from peer collaboration, in which both parties participate in each other's learning on a relatively equal footing and cooperative learning in which each child takes on one aspect of a group task.

While all three processes can play a part in the education of a child with Down's Syndrome in the mainstream, it is peer tutoring that will be examined in some depth here. Research on peer tutoring indicates that children involved in the tutoring role (Foot *et al.*, 1990) may:

- gain a deeper understanding of the material learned by having to teach it
- increase in maturity, sense of responsibility, sensitivity, concern and empathy for others
- enhance self-esteem, self-confidence and levels of aspiration
- develop prosocial behaviours and better social skills.

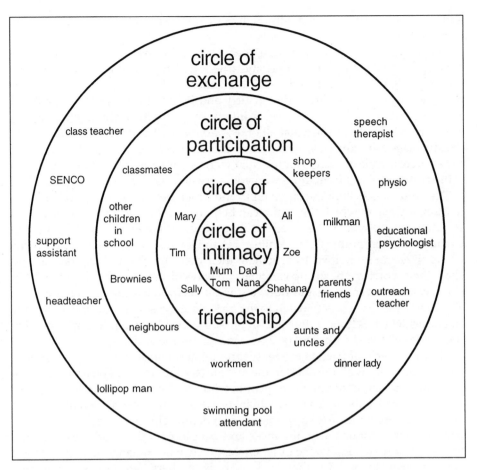

Figure 8.4 A circle of friends

Gains for the child being tutored are also apparent. Schools involved in the process report positive effects all round, as long as the programme is well structured and organised, and tutors are properly trained.

Students being tutored by peers (Ashman and Elkins, 1990) gain from the:

- individualised instruction
- positive effects of modelling
- use of tangible rewards to increase motivation
- potency of a peer as a means of providing instruction and reinforcement.

Regular peer tutoring also gives opportunities for increased social interaction which might not otherwise occur.

While most reported uses of peer tutoring concentrate on the development of reading or spelling in low performing children without specific disabilities, there are a few studies which include children with Down's Syndrome. Cooke *et al.* (1982) describe the inclusion of a seven-year-old girl with Down's Syndrome in a daily peer tutoring programme in a first grade classroom, using same age classmates. The programme consisted of three phases as outlined below.

1. The tutor huddle, in which the tutors tested each other on the words they would be teaching that day. Tutors each held an envelope of GO words which the children they were tutoring would be working on.
2. The practice session, lasting five minutes. Each word in the envelope was presented once and a standard prompting procedure used. At the first error, the tutor said 'Try again'. At the second error they gave the word 'Say——' and their partner repeated it. Intermittent praise was used throughout the session.
3. Testing, where each word was tested and a smiley face or X drawn on the back of the card.

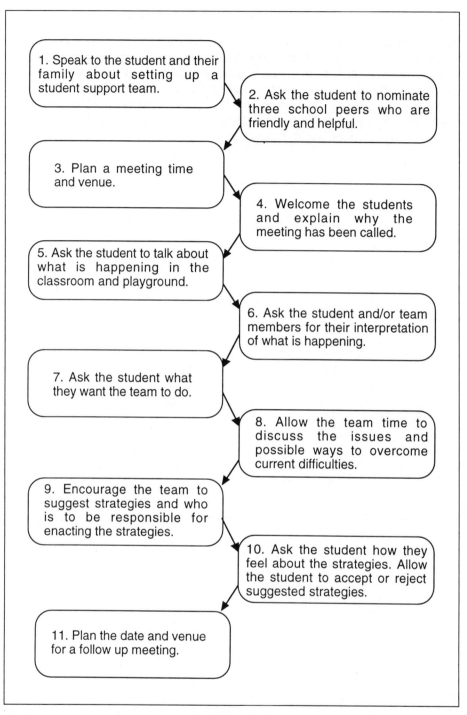

Figure 8.5 Building a student support team

Words were left in the GO pocket until they had been given smiley faces on three consecutive occasions. They were then moved to a STOP pocket. Once a week, STOP words were re-presented and if failed, were replaced in the GO pocket for recycling. Correctly read words were removed from the system and new words introduced when the GO pocket was empty.

In evaluating the programme for Joanne, the student with Down's Syndrome, significant gains were noted. However, the following modifications were recommended.

1. Reducing the number of words in the GO pocket from 10 to 5.

2. Training tutors in strategies to deal with off-task behaviour.

While there are few, if any, reports of peer tutoring with students with Down's Syndrome in this country, there seems no reason why same-age peers, or older students such as sixth formers, could not be used to work on a range of basic skills, supplementing the work of the support assistant or class teacher.

The prompt spelling programme described by Watkins and Hunter-Carsch (1995) would appear to be one that could be adapted to meet the needs of secondary-aged students with Down's Syndrome.

Chapter 9

Working with Parents and with Outside Agencies

As Gross (1996) notes:

> This is the age of parent power. Like it or not, gone are the days when parents expected professionals in school to do their job without asking too much about how they did it or what it was reasonable to expect from the system. Now, in education as in other areas, parents are expected to act as consumers exercising choice and evaluating the product.

For the majority of parents of a child with Down's Syndrome, fighting the system has become a way of life by the time the child reaches school age. Increasingly, parents of children with Down's Syndrome are seeking a mainstream placement for their children as this is seen as the most effective means by which they can be accepted into the local community. Yet experience suggests that the majority of professionals in Health, Education and Social Services still see the child's disability first and the child second. Although few families have any difficulty in accessing specialist services, they are, almost invariably, left to explore mainstream options on their own with neither encouragement nor practical help.

Parents who refuse a hospital-based special play group or a place in the nursery class of the local special school are often considered to be unreasonable and unable to accept their child's disability. Parents who prefer to keep their young child at home are seen as denying them the benefits of special help, although the evidence to support early professional input is far from decisive. Despite assurances from the LEA that an early special school placement will not pre-empt any decision regarding placement at five, many parents who take this route find themselves unable to gain a mainstream placement once their child reaches school age. Rather than being seen as a pointer towards inclusion, the child's progress is used as evidence of the appropriateness of the special school.

Preliminary results from a nation-wide survey being carried out by the author indicate that more than a quarter of parents who gain a mainstream placement for their child with Down's Syndrome have to fight to achieve this. Many parents are having to resort to the SEN Tribunal while others simply give up in the face of long-term concerted opposition from LEA officers, educational psychologists or local schools. One parent reports having to find a different junior school after a successful experience in the feeder infant school, after the junior headteacher, who had no direct experience of her child, stated that they 'had neither the expertise nor the resources'.

Many LEAs, while willing to provide support, are not prepared to advise parents about particular schools or put pressure on headteachers to accept children with Down's Syndrome. The law is clear that the responsibility for naming a school lies with the LEA. Even so, individual schools are too often being allowed to call the tune. Certainly, parents are clear that a positive response from the school is essential if their child is to succeed in the mainstream.

Nevertheless, some schools have admitted that only by working with the child and the family have they been able to overcome their prejudices and realise

Partnership with parents

79

the benefits of inclusive education. One primary head, directed by his LEA to accept a child with Down's Syndrome, told the author that he did everything in his power to avoid admitting the child, but failed to overturn the LEA's direction. Some seven years later, he commented in a conversation with the author, who was then his educational psychologist, that it was the best thing that had ever happened to the school and, in his opinion, every mainstream school should be made to do the same.

In attempting to establish a positive relationship with the parents of a child with Down's Syndrome, schools must not be surprised to be faced with parents who are wary, apprehensive, demanding or even somewhat aggressive at times. Initially, parents may seek a high level of involvement with the school and may need to check on their child's progress on a daily basis. However, once the child has settled, an agreed programme of weekly, monthly or termly meetings should be arranged and the parents encouraged to hand over day-to-day responsibility. A home/school diary can be a useful form of communication, particularly where parents are anxious or problems are occurring.

Some teachers, already under pressure, find the presence of a child with Down's Syndrome in their class a major cause of stress. Where this is not recognised by the headteacher and appropriate support offered, it can result in friction between the teacher and the parents. Parents, taking a genuine interest in their child's progress and wishing to achieve the best possible outcomes, may be perceived as pushy and overdemanding. On the other hand, a teacher under stress may be seen as uninterested and prejudiced against the child. Where such situations exist, it is imperative that a neutral figure from the school, the LEA or a voluntary organisation attempts to resolve the dispute, or the child will undoubtedly suffer.

Parental involvement in their child's learning can be particularly helpful for the student with Down's Syndrome. Many parents will already have experience of working with their child on a one-to-one basis and will be keer to continue. A common approach to reading, writing or maths will be helpful, both to the parent and to the child, and parents will often appreciate being given access to materials brought into school by advisory staff or therapists. Frequently, however, it is the parents who have access to the most up-to-date information. It is important that teachers do not perceive this as interference, but welcome any additional ideas or teaching materials that the parents might be prepared to share.

Where the child is behaving inappropriately, it is important that a behavioural strategy is established in cooperation with the parents. Frequently, a discussion will reveal the cause of the problem and allow school staff to devise appropriate interventions. In other cases, it may be necessary to involve an educational psychologist or advisory teacher in developing a programme that can be used both in school and at home. Where mainstream placements have broken down, it is often because problems have not been addressed at an early stage and parents have not been involved until it was too late to intervene effectively.

In working with parents of children with Down's Syndrome the guidelines outlined in Figure 9.1 are recommended.

The role of the speech therapist

The involvement of paramedical professionals is likely to continue at some level after the child starts school. However, hospital or clinic sessions may be reduced in frequency or even stopped. Instead, therapists may take on a monitoring or training function. Results from the author's current survey suggest that less than 30% of students with Down's Syndrome in mainstream schools see a speech therapist more than once a term. Approximately 38 per cent of primary-aged children receive a termly monitoring visit although this type of input is rarely

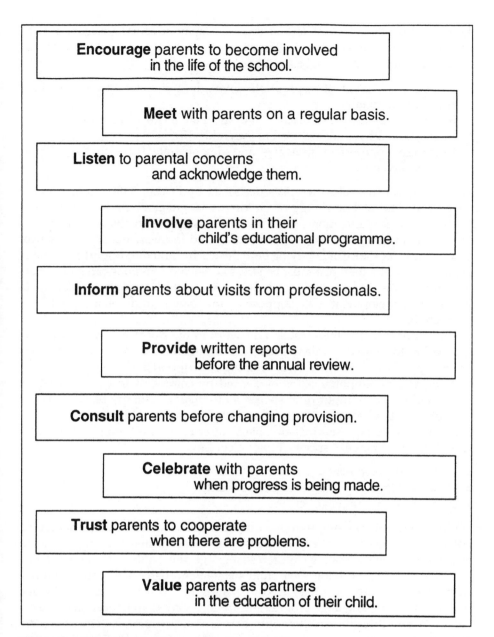

Encourage parents to become involved in the life of the school.

Meet with parents on a regular basis.

Listen to parental concerns and acknowledge them.

Involve parents in their child's educational programme.

Inform parents about visits from professionals.

Provide written reports before the annual review.

Consult parents before changing provision.

Celebrate with parents when progress is being made.

Trust parents to cooperate when there are problems.

Value parents as partners in the education of their child.

Figure 9.1 Working in partnership with parents

offered at secondary level. In the survey 33 per cent of primary and 68 per cent of secondary parents report that their child receives no regular support from a speech and language therapist.

Whatever the pattern of support offered, it is important that schools liaise with those concerned and ensure that an appropriate level of input is retained. One of the problems in the delivery of an effective service to children with Down's Syndrome in mainstream schools is a difference in perception of the child's needs between the therapist, the school staff and often the parents. Some children with Down's Syndrome clearly require structured input from a therapist to deal with severe articulation problems or to establish basic signing skills. However, for the majority, it is the provision of an appropriate language environment and the delivery of structured language programmes, in class or in a group setting, that is more important.

Experience has shown that these can be provided very effectively by a support teacher or learning support assistant who has developed a good relationship with the child. Despite a lack of formal training, many support assistants already possess a range of relevant skills. The role of the speech and language therapist should, therefore be three-fold as outlined below.

1. To assess the child at appropriate intervals and determine the type of intervention required.
2. To liaise with the class teacher and the parents to ensure that relevant language objectives are included in the child's IEP.
3. To design appropriate strategies and demonstrate these to the support assistant involved.

In carrying out this role, therapists described by Dobson (1995) relied on the support assistants' knowledge of children's language skills to evaluate the effectiveness of interventions. They also used assistants to observe and record children's language in the classroom setting and in interactions with the peer group. The importance of involving both the teacher and the support assistant in planning with the therapist must be stressed. Such discussions can help school staff realise the importance of whole school and classroom approaches to language development, as opposed to more traditional one-to-one interventions.

Where possible, the therapist should work in the classroom, demonstrating approaches to be used. While written programmes are useful as a back-up, they are rarely sufficient on their own. Training for support assistants is clearly an issue of national importance, as evidenced by comments in the latest Green Paper (DfEE 1997b). Input from speech and language therapy services should undoubtedly form a key component of such training. In addition, some speech and language therapy services are able to offer in-service training (INSET) for school staff on a range of specific topics including:

- language development and Down's Syndrome
- Makaton, Signalong or other signing systems
- the Derbyshire Language Scheme.

While face-to-face therapy from a qualified speech and language therapist is not necessary in the majority of cases, it is essential that a therapist retains responsibility for overseeing children's language development throughout their school career. On receiving their child's statement, parents of young children with Down's Syndrome are advised to ensure that speech therapy advice and the provision of a language programme are included as an educational need in Part 3. Where therapy is written into Part 6 of an exisiting statement as non-educational provision, parents can ask the LEA to amend Part 3 following an annual review.

Legal precedents have already been set (R vs. Lancashire County Council *ex parte* M, 1989), which confirm that where language development is an essential component of learning, as in Down's Syndrome, the need is clearly educational. Yet many LEAs are still trying to avoid their legal responsibilities by blaming the lack of provision on the health authority. Comments in the Government's latest Green Paper (DfEE, 1997b) indicate that this distinction is likely to be removed in the near future and LEAs made jointly responsible for the provision of speech therapy for all children. Hopefully, this should end the disputes and improve the level of provision overall.

The learning support teacher

The main concern of many classroom teachers, catering for a child with Down's Syndrome for the first time is whether they are doing the right thing. Teachers worry that:

- they haven't been trained to teach such children
- they haven't got the time to give the child enough special help
- the child will be missing out on the expertise of the special school
- they are not sure how to use the support assistant to best effect.

Many of these worries are unfounded. However, the reassurance offered by regular visits from a learning support teacher can be invaluable in establishing good practice and building staff confidence. Regrettably, in a sample of children with Down's Syndrome in the author's survey, only 28 per cent were in schools which had regular visits from an advisory teacher. Overall, 18 per cent of children in the sample received termly visits, while a further 10 per cent were seen several times a term. In the majority of instances, this support came from a local authority advisory or learning support service.

Shotter (1997), an outreach teacher from Devon, describes in some detail the way in which such support can help both children and schools (see Figures 9.2 and 9.3). As a teacher specialising in the education of children with Down's Syndrome, she is able to work intensively with a small group of schools. In many ways her role is that of an Inclusion Facilitator.

Sadly, few LEAs offer this type of dedicated service. However, in many areas, teachers from more generic support services carry out many of the same functions, to good effect. Certainly there is no evidence that teachers carrying out this role need to have direct experience of teaching children with Down's Syndrome. Special needs teachers with skills in differentiation and knowledge of good practice in inclusive education can soon gain the specific knowledge they need, through reading or by attending focused INSET.

Of greater importance are listening skills, and the ability to work collaboratively and build confidence. It is these skills that need to be developed if special school teachers are to take on an advisory and outreach role, as envisaged in the latest Green Paper (DfEE, 1997b). While many special school teachers are highly skilled in working with small groups or with individual children, they may not have sufficient knowledge or experience of mainstream settings to demonstrate good inclusive practice.

Techniques used successfully in the special school may not translate into the mainstream setting at all or may require regular withdrawal of the child from normal lessons. Teachers, if not handled sensitively, may feel de-skilled by the undoubted expertise of some special school staff and be more inclined to abdicate their responsibility for the child. Notwithstanding, some special schools have developed highly effective outreach arms with staff trained in the support role. Where there is a real commitment to inclusion these services can work well.

The educational psychologist

The role of the educational psychologist has changed quite markedly in recent years. In most LEAs, there has been a relentless increase in the number of statutory assessments to be completed. Further, the Government's imposition of predetermined time limits for assessment has left psychologists with little opportunity to work preventatively or support schools in the development of good practice. As the Green Paper (DfEE, 1997b) notes:

Educational psychologists employed by LEAs have wide responsibilities. But a large part of their time is tied up in the process of statutory assessment. While this may be necessary in some cases, it diverts key resources from early intervention and from providing help and support to pupils when it is most needed.

Despite the pressure of work, educational psychologists are increasingly committed to inclusive education and in many areas of the country are

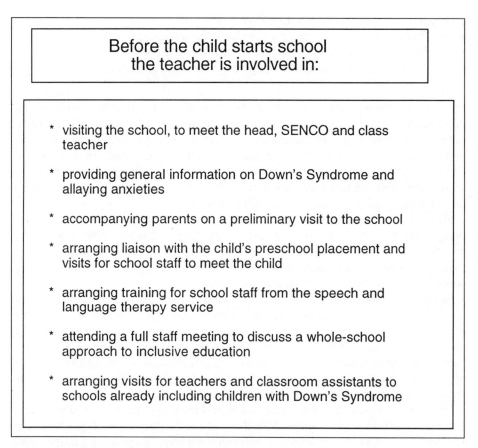

Before the child starts school the teacher is involved in:

* visiting the school, to meet the head, SENCO and class teacher

* providing general information on Down's Syndrome and allaying anxieties

* accompanying parents on a preliminary visit to the school

* arranging liaison with the child's preschool placement and visits for school staff to meet the child

* arranging training for school staff from the speech and language therapy service

* attending a full staff meeting to discuss a whole-school approach to inclusive education

* arranging visits for teachers and classroom assistants to schools already including children with Down's Syndrome

Figure 9.2 The role of the outreach teacher (1)

cooperating with teachers in developing whole-school approaches. Most of the training offered by LEAs for support assistants – e.g. in Wiltshire, Leeds and Northumberland (Clayton, 1990, Lorenz, 1992, Caswell and Pinner, 1996) – has been developed by the psychological service. Psychologists in Derbyshire developed the Derbyshire Language Scheme (Knowles and Masidlover, 1982). More recently, the use of Circles of Friends has gained widespread acceptance through the work of educational psychologists in Nottinghamshire (Wilson and Newton, 1996). More specifically in the area of Down's Syndrome, Jane Beadman, an educational psychologist, has produced a whole range of training resources for teachers and learning support assistants in mainstream schools. (These are published by DLR – see Appendix 2 for address.)

In the Green Paper (DfEE, 1997b), a commitment is made 'to explore ways of changing the balance of work of EPs [educational psychologists], so that they can use their expertise as productively as possible'.

In the near future, therefore, schools should be able to call on their educational psychologist to perform a far wider range of duties (see Figure 9.4).

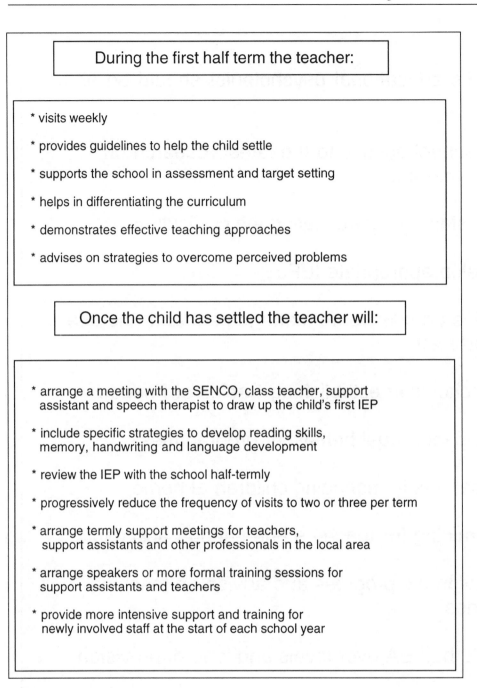

During the first half term the teacher:

* visits weekly

* provides guidelines to help the child settle

* supports the school in assessment and target setting

* helps in differentiating the curriculum

* demonstrates effective teaching approaches

* advises on strategies to overcome perceived problems

Once the child has settled the teacher will:

* arrange a meeting with the SENCO, class teacher, support assistant and speech therapist to draw up the child's first IEP

* include specific strategies to develop reading skills, memory, handwriting and language development

* review the IEP with the school half-termly

* progressively reduce the frequency of visits to two or three per term

* arrange termly support meetings for teachers, support assistants and other professionals in the local area

* arrange speakers or more formal training sessions for support assistants and teachers

* provide more intensive support and training for newly involved staff at the start of each school year

Figure 9.3 The role of the outreach teacher (2)

The school's educational psychologist should be able to:

* give the school access to the latest research on Down's Syndrome

* work with staff on differentiating the curriculum

* help develop appropriate IEPs

* give advice on classroom management and the use of support staff

* support schools in establishing Circles of Friends

* help set up individual behaviour programmes

* support parents in managing children at home

* provide training for teachers and support assistants

* review children's progress and advise on teaching approaches

* liaise with the LEA over levels and type of provision

* liaise with the health authority over speech or occupational therapy

* liaise with Social Services over community based support.

Figure 9.4 The role of the educational psychologist

Chapter 10

A Vision for the Future

As David Blunkett, Secretary of State for Education and Employment, states in the Foreword to the latest Green Paper (DfEE, 1997b) 'Where all children are included as equal partners in the school community, the benefits are felt by all.'

However, if the opportunity of receiving a high-quality education in a local mainstream school is to be made available to all children with Down's Syndrome, much still needs to be done. The Alliance for Inclusive Education (1997), in its response to the Green Paper, outlines some of the changes that need to be achieved. Most of these are discussed in the rest of this chapter.

A need for change

The existing law, with its three caveats, gives LEAs ample opportunity to deny parents of children with special needs the right to a place in a mainstream school. Yet if these same conditions were applied to children without statements, significant numbers might be without a place in a mainstream school. Despite the inability of some schools to provide an appropriately challenging curriculum, highly gifted students are not refused entry even though 'the provision required to meet their needs' is unavailable. Similarly, students recently arrived in this country with no grasp of English are not denied places in mainstream schools, even where there is no second language expertise available.

If a mainstream place was denied to every student whose presence in a mainstream school was 'incompatible with the provision of efficient education for the children with whom he would be educated', there would be even more children out of school than there are at present. Schools are expressly denied the right to refuse entry to students with a history of difficult or disruptive behaviour and have to provide extensive evidence before they are permitted to exclude permanently. Yet the same schools are able to refuse entry to a student with a statement if they believe his or her presence will adversely affect others. This is convenient for those who wish to discriminate against children with learning disabilities.

Finally, no LEA is expected to ensure the 'efficient use of resources' in the case of children without statements. Any school that attempted to refuse entry to a child being 'looked after' by Social Services, because the additional staff time required to attend case conferences and liaise with social workers would constitute an unreasonable drain on their budget, would be pilloried in the press. Yet children with disabilities are denied mainstream places for just this reason. Unless the 1993 Education Act is amended, to give the same rights to all parents, there will always be some parts of the country in which children with Down's Syndrome will be denied an inclusive education. As the Green Paper (DfEE, 1997b) states: 'There is no reason why children with similar needs in different parts of the country should not have similar opportunities to attend mainstream schools'.

While the recent Green Paper supports the Salamanca Statement on inclusive education (UNESCO, 1994) it fails to mention the 1989 UN Convention on the

Changing the law

Rights of the Child or the 1993 UN Standard Rules on the Equalisation of Opportunities for Persons with Disabilities, to which this country is also a signatory (Wertheimer, 1997). Article 12 of the UN Convention affirms each child's right to express an opinion and have that opinion taken into account in any matter or procedure affecting them. Similarly, the Children Act (1989) stresses the need to consider: 'the ascertainable wishes and feelings of the child concerned' before any decisions are made regarding his or her upbringing. Nevertheless, education law concerns itself only with the rights of parents. While most parents have the best interests of their children at heart, this is not always the case. Short-term advantages of special schooling, such as the provision of free transport or the availability of speech and physiotherapy in the school, may outweigh the longer-term benefits of mainstream provision.

Although we may acknowledge the distress experienced and expressed by young people separated from their friends and sent away to a special school at age 11, there is no way at present of ensuring that it is taken into consideration when placement decisions are being made. If we are not to discriminate against children with special educational needs, it is important that we start listening to them and find better ways of determining their true concerns and feelings. Attempts must also be made to incorporate key aspects of the Children Act into educational legislation.

Improving provision

One of the major stumbling blocks to effective inclusion is the lack of appropriate provision in some areas of the country. Where LEAs have invested heavily in their special schools there is often little money left to support students in the mainstream. The delegation of special needs budgets to schools has resulted in the decimation of many LEA support services, and with them has gone the ability of the LEA to offer comprehensive programmes of training for teachers and support assistants. Authorities with highly segregated systems will be less willing to explore more inclusive options, such as the development of resourced or focused high schools, for fear that special school places will be left empty.

The LEAs' problems of double funding have now been recognised by the Government, and in the Green Paper (DfEE, 1997b) they talk of: 'providing pump-priming support to LEAs which commit themselves to greater levels of inclusion, to assist with transitional costs of running both mainstream and special school provision.'.

They also discuss a change in role for existing special schools, from separate institutions concerned only with their own pupils to more open centres of excellence offering to advise and support mainstream colleagues. While this sounds admirable, such initiatives need to be viewed with some caution.

Firstly, it gives validity to the largely unsubstantiated belief that there exists within special schools a technology of instruction that is special and different from that in the mainstream. Yet we know that the essence of good teaching is the same whatever the setting. Further, it assumes that special school staff are all additionally qualified However, many teachers in special schools have had no specialised training. On the other hand, many mainstream SENCOs and support teachers have impressive qualifications in the teaching and management of students with special educational needs.

Teachers working in schools for children with learning difficulties may have no experience of the mainstream or may have moved into a special school well before all the changes brought about by the last Government were fully implemented. They may then be in a very poor position to advise on appropriate methodology to increase inclusion, particularly if they still believe strongly in the benefits of special schooling. Even where they support the inclusion initiative, they may have few advisory skills and may require extensive retraining.

If more mainstream schools are to be encouraged to take on board the education of children with Down's Syndrome, it is vital that they have access to accurate and up-to-date information. They need to be shown examples of good practice in other schools and given opportunities to discuss issues with colleagues in schools where inclusion is a reality. Mel Ainscow at Manchester University and Judy Sebba at the Cambridge Institute of Education coordinate a network of inclusive secondary schools that are linked to share experiences and improve their practice. In addition, CSIE is building up a database of inclusive primary and secondary schools, which interested parties are welcome to consult.

Information and training

Information regarding the positive impact of students with special needs on exam performance in inclusive schools would help overcome the fear of some heads and governors that their reputation, and hence their enrolment, would be adversely affected by the admission of a student with Down's Syndrome. Newham, the LEA with the lowest level of segregated special educational provision (Norwich, 1997), is also the authority with the highest rate of improvement in exam performance (Pyke, 1997).

Training for SENCOs, class teachers and learning support assistants is vital if inclusive education is to benefit students with Down's Syndrome. New organisations such as CLASS (the Confederation of Learning Assistants with Specialist Skills) stress the need for nationally recognised and accredited training for all support assistants and this theme is taken up in the Green Paper (DfEE, 1997b). However, as Moyles (1997) points out, it is not only support assistants who need appropriate training:

> While the Specialist Teacher Assistant courses and increased numbers of support staff has generally raised awareness of the training needs of classroom assistants, the training needs of teachers in working with assistants has received little consideration by schools or training providers. Many teachers and Headteachers acknowledge the vital need of teachers for some training themselves, in leading and managing what is now amounting to potentially a large number of variously trained (and untrained) adults working with them in the classroom consistently and spasmodically throughout the week.

In reviewing the SEN-related training required by headteachers, SENCOs, experienced classroom teachers and those in training, the Teacher Training Agency needs to take on board the issue of inclusion in general, as well as focusing on more traditional areas of special educational need such as the Code of Practice, early identification and assessment and the differentiation of the curriculum. The advantages of mixed-ability teaching for students with learning difficulties also need to be stressed, despite the government's expressed preference for setting, together with the skills required to make it effective for all students.

Finally, some attention should be paid to the development of training initiatives in the use of peer support and the establishment of Circles of Friends. While peer tutoring gained considerable popularity in the 1970s and 80s, it seems to have been abandoned in many LEAs. As schools throughout the country are being encouraged to focus on raising standards in literacy, large numbers of children would benefit from its revival. Circle Time, on the other hand, appears to be gaining a large following in many authorities. This interest could usefully be harnessed by support services in developing the use of peers to improve inclusive practices.

Parental involvement

Despite the growing support for inclusive education in general and for the inclusion of children with Down's Syndrome in particular, all concerned accept that parents have a right to choose. In exercising that right, many parents will need support. The success of the government-funded Parent Partnership programme has now been established (Wolfendale, 1997). Although the current round of government funding has come to an end, the Green Paper (DfEE, 1997b) makes a commitment that by the year 2002:

> All parents whose children are being assessed for a statement of SEN will be offered the support of an independent 'Named Person'. Parent partnership programmes will be in place in every LEA in England and will play an important part in supporting parents of children with SEN.

Many Parent Support Schemes have been highly effective. However, the independence of some has been brought into question. By channelling grant money through LEAs, the government has accepted that many would appoint their own employees to partnership posts. Perceived conflicts of interest have deterred some parents from seeking help in appealing against LEA decisions. In other cases the Parent Partnership Officers themselves have felt constrained in offering impartial advice.

As the Alliance for Inclusive Education (1997) states:

> Parent Partnership Schemes should be independent from LEAs and run by and accountable to users, with input from the voluntary sector at local level. Grassroots work at school level will lead to good practice when early intervention is based on trust.

Unless such schemes are truly independent, parents will continue to seek support from already overstretched charities such as the Down's Syndrome Association, IPSEA (the Independent Panel for Special Educational Advice) or Network 81 (see Appendix 2 for addresses). With support, parents who hope to gain a mainstream place for their child will persevere and by so doing will often overcome the resistance of schools and LEAs. All concerned are then given the chance to experience real success, as in the case of one young man who transferred from a special school to the mainstream at the age of nine (Churchill, 1993).

> Looking back over the past two terms in which Daniel has been with us, I feel that his transfer into mainstream school has been an exciting and successful venture. His own cheerful and amenable personality has been a major factor in enabling him to settle into a new environment with the minimum of fuss...His parents have commented that he seems to have acquired a higher degree of personal dignity and confidence, and he certainly seems happy and at ease at school. Progress is not a steadily rising line, but a series of steps and plateaus of consolidation. Daniel has undoubtedly learned a great deal from this experience, as have all of us in the school, and we feel it has been very worth while.

Case Histories

Martin is now six years old and is a member of a Year 1 class in a local mainstream school, with children a year younger than he is. The second of two boys, he attended playgroup from the age of three. Additional support was offered by Social Services who provided the salary for a support assistant with signing skills for three mornings a week. Despite a significant language delay, Martin was not offered regular speech therapy by the health authority. The family therefore approached their fund-holding GP who arranged for fortnightly therapy to be provided for Martin at home.

Martin

Martin enjoyed playgroup and progressed well. At the age of three-and-a-half he received a statement from the LEA which recommended placement in a school for pupils with severe learning difficulties. He started attending the special school for two mornings a week, while continuing at playgroup for the remaining three. However, it soon became clear that while progress continued to be made at playgroup the special school sessions caused him to regress and become increasingly withdrawn. After a term his parents decided to remove him from the special school and increase his time at playgroup.

At the age of four-and-a-half Martin was reassessed and a place offered at a unit for children with moderate learning difficulties some distance from his home. His parents visited the unit, but were concerned about the wide age range in the class and the limited amount of integration offered. They declined the place and decided to appeal. In the interim Martin, although now of school age, remained at playgroup. Since Social Service funding was no longer available, the parents had to meet the cost of the support assistant themselves.

At Tribunal, the parents requested a part-time place in the Nursery class of a local mainstream primary school, with a transfer to the Reception class the following September. They won their appeal and Martin was admitted to the school of their choice on a half-time basis with ten hours support. At the age of five-and-three-quarters he transferred to Reception and his support was increased to 16 hours and 15 minutes.

His support assistant was trained in Makaton signing and, in addition, Martin was offered weekly speech therapy in school. Martin has settled extremely well and has made dramatic progress in language skills. The school is extremely positive and notes real gains, both academically and socially. His parents still feel sad that it was necessary for them to go to appeal and to deny Martin a year of schooling. Nevertheless, they are sure that the fight was worthwhile.

Robbie is now nine and attends a local junior school with children of his own age. The youngest of seven children in a large supportive family, Robbie was offered special education from the age of two. This the family refused as they preferred to work with him at home. At the age of three his formal assessment was completed by the LEA and he was admitted to the Nursery class of his local first school with full-time support. Although the support was subsequently reduced to

Robbie

ten hours, he coped well in Nursery and transferred to Reception with his peers.

Because of some initial problems in the playground, Robbie's mother was asked to come into school to supervise him during afternoon break. This she continued to do on a daily basis for two years, although there were no further problems. The following September Robbie moved into a mixed Reception/Year 1 class. While he continued to make good progress and presented no behaviour problems, it soon became clear that the ten hours support offered was not considered sufficient by the school, despite the additional provision of two-and-a-half hours teacher time and regular speech therapy. At every opportunity the head reiterated his belief that the school 'was not meeting his needs'.

Following an annual review, Robbie's statement was amended to name a school for pupils with severe learning difficulties. The parents objected and submitted an appeal to the local Appeals Committee. Pending the appeal the LEA increased his support to 20 hours. However, the school Governors insisted that he was taken home at 3 p.m. each day when his support assistant finished work. At the end of his time in Year 1, the school decided that he could not transfer with his friends into Year 2. Instead he was moved back to the Reception class.

His parents' appeal was heard by the local Appeals Committee who recommended a reassessment of Robbie's needs. This was carried out but confirmed the earlier recommendation for placement in a school for pupils with severe learning difficulties. The parents again appealed, this time to the SEN Tribunal. Before the hearing Robbie moved class again, this time into mixed Reception/Year 1, although he was now seven-and-a-half. In addition, his nursery nurse was directed to spend three mornings a week with him in the nursery.

The second appeal was heard by the SEN Tribunal and confirmed the appropriateness of his mainstream placement. While the attitude of the school improved somewhat following the appeal, the family decided to move to a new LEA before he was due to transfer to middle school, to avoid further conflict. His new authority has been very positive and he was admitted to a local mainstream school with 20 hours' support. While it is still early days he seems to have settled well.

Serena

Serena is 12 and is the second of four children. She attended a Social Services Day Nursery with her older brother and then transferred to the Reception class of her local primary school shortly before her fifth birthday. A full-time support assistant was appointed for 32 hours and 30 minutes each week. A proportion of this time was used for joint planning with the class teacher.

Both the school and the parents were delighted with Serena's progress and each year she moved up with her friends. By the time she reached Year 6 she was by no means the poorest reader in the class and was working independently for much of the time. Her support assistant was always available although she spent much of her time helping other children, responding to Serena only when she asked for help.

In the November of Serena's final primary year an annual review was held in school attended by the educational psychologist as well as the parents and school staff. At that meeting it was agreed that she would move on to the adjacent grant-maintained high school to which her brother had transferred the previous year. The parents duly applied for a place which was offered on condition that appropriate levels of support were forthcoming.

The parents continued to liaise with both the primary and the high school, but nothing further was heard from the LEA until the end of March when an amended statement was issued naming a special school for pupils with moderate learning difficulties. The parents duly visited the school named, despite their major reservations about special education and were concerned to discover that it catered only for pupils up to the age of 12, necessitating a further move after a year to another special school which they also visited. Neither school, offered an appropriate peer group or a sufficiently challenging curriculum. The parents, therefore, decided to appeal to the SEN Tribunal.

Their appeal was heard as Serena was about to leave her primary school. At the appeal the LEA was unable to provide any evidence regarding the unsuitability of the high school. Nevertheless, they convinced the Tribunal Panel that her needs would best be met in a special school and the parents lost their appeal. Serena is now being educated at home while her parents prepare a case for the High Court.

Daniel

Daniel, now aged 14, is the younger of two boys. He attended a special nursery until he was three and then transferred to the Nursery class of a local school on a part-time basis. When he reached school age, it was agreed that he would spend an extra year in the nursery attending on a full-time basis. He did well at nursery and then transferred to the Reception class of a school nearer his home which did not have a nursery of its own. While the headteacher was very apprehensive about admitting a child with Down's Syndrome, the LEA was encouraging and offered full-time support from a nursery nurse.

Daniel progressed steadily up the school with the support of his teachers and his nursery nurse. However, the head was never convinced that he was appropriately placed and regularly sought confirmation from professionals that Daniel would be better off 'with his own kind' in a special school. Fortunately, no one took any notice and he completed his primary education without undue problems.

Prior to secondary transfer the parents visited the local high school. While they were greeted positively they felt that Daniel would be a guinea pig in a school without the necessary level of expertise. Therefore, they chose to send him to another high school approximately five miles from his home which had been additionally resourced for pupils with severe learning difficulties (SLD). In each year group there are approximately four SLD pupils. At the point at which Daniel was admitted, the school already had some six years' experience of similar pupils.

Daniel is now in a Year 9 form group with pupils a year younger than himself. He is taught in mixed ability classes for geography, history, technology, RE, art, science and French with in-class support from one of a team of special needs assistants. English, maths and supplementary studies are delivered in the Resource Base by a highly experienced special needs teacher who has overall responsibility for pupils with severe learning difficulties. In addition to the normal curriculum she offers independence training and covers areas such as sex education in a small group of pupils at a similar level of maturity. A speech therapist visits termly to review his programme.

Daniel is doing well and has made friends both with ordinary students and with others who experience similar learning difficulties. His parents believe that he has had the best of both worlds.

Philip

Philip is 15. The middle of three children, he attended his local playgroup without additional support and appeared to be doing well. His parents approached the LEA seeking a mainstream school. While the LEA was positive, relatively few schools at that time had experience of children with Down's Syndrome. Since the local school was less than enthusiastic, the parents were directed to a school some four miles from home which had already worked successfully with another similar child.

Half-time support from a nursery nurse was offered initially while Philip attended the nursery class on a full-time basis. However, this was increased to full-time when he moved into Reception. Because of the distance, he was taken to school by taxi. This caused some problems in the establishment of close home/school links and communication tended to be by telephone. Similarly, it was harder for him to make local friends. Nevertheless he did well and moved up the school with his peers. At the age of 11 he invited everyone in his class to his birthday party and they all came, to the consternation of his parents who had not anticipated such an overwhelming response.

In Philip's final year, the parents approached the local high school already attended by his sister. It was extremely positive and he transferred with everyone's blessing. The school was offered support from a special needs assistant for up to 75 per cent of the week and additional teacher time for the remaining 25 per cent. In the early years the teacher time was used for the preparation of materials. Latterly it has been used for direct teaching in a small group. Philip is now in Year 11 and he has done remarkably well. He is placed in lower sets for science and maths, and in mixed ability groups for English, drama, and PE. His basic curriculum is supplemented by eight periods of life skills each week. To allow time for this he no longer takes French or German.

In-class support is offered on a very flexible basis in response to Philip's needs and those of subject teachers. No additional support is provided at break or lunchtime, although he has his friends around him. While the attitude of some staff could still be improved, the vast majority have been supportive and encouraging. Philip's parents have no doubt that he has benefited in both the academic and the social sense from attending a local mainstream school. Although the school had no prior experience of children with Down's Syndrome, they had been including students with physical disabilities for some time. It seems likely that by so doing they developed positive attitudes and teaching approaches which benefited all students.

Grace

Grace is now 18 and is working as a trainee in an organisation supporting people with learning disabilities in the community. The younger of two children, she attended an Opportunity Playgroup from the age of two and then transferred to a local nursery school, which she attended full-time until she started school. Because she was very small for her age and was summer-born, she stayed at nursery for an extra term and then moved into school a year behind her peers.

Whilst at nursery she was a regular visitor to the primary school attended by her brother and so she was well-known at the school by the time she started in Reception. Formal assessment had been completed before she started school, but no additional resources were offered. Despite the lack of support, the school was welcoming and she settled well. After two terms the school and parents approached the LEA for additional help which eventually was forthcoming, She then moved through the primary school with 16 hours 15 minutes support from a nursery nurse. By the age of 11 Grace was speaking and reading fluently, and had made many friends.

The initial plan was for her to transfer to the same high school as her brother. However, Grace had other ideas and insisted on going to secondary school with her friends. Fortunately, the new school was happy to accept her even though the LEA was only prepared to offer five hours' additional support. Generally, things went well although there were periods of bullying by a few less able boys who resented her having extra help. Problems came to a head following a debate on abortion, when the example used was a baby with Down's Syndrome. However, she learned to cope.

By the age of 14 she had a reading age of 17 and in Year 10 she started studying for GCSEs. At that point an extra 10 hours of support was provided and she was entered for English Language, English Literature, Geography, Science, Maths, Child Care and Keyboard Skills. She failed her Maths but passed the remaining six subjects with grades ranging from C–E. She then moved on to college to complete an NVQ Level 2 in Business and Administration.

Grace is now an attractive and well-adjusted young lady with an active social life. She has had several boyfriends but is by no means ready for a serious relationship. She has been taking driving lessons, but is not sure that she trusts the behaviour of other drivers on the road. She hopes in the near future to leave home and share a house with her best friend. Her real ambition is to write a book about what it's like to have Down's syndrome.

Useful Addresses

Alliance for Inclusive Education
Unit 2
70 South Lambeth Road
LONDON
SW8 1RL
Tel: 0171 735 5277

AMS Educational
Woodside Trading Estate
Law Lane
Horsforth
LEEDS
LS18 5NY
Tel: 0113 258 0309

Centre for Studies on Inclusive Education (CSIE)
1 Redland Close
Elm Lane
Redland
BRISTOL
BS6 6UE
Tel: 0117 923 8450

Circles Network
Pamwell House
160 Pennywell Road
Upper Easton
BRISTOL
BS5 0TX
Tel: 0117 939 6660

Confederation of Learning Assistants with Specialist Skills (CLASS)
83 Maple Road
Dartford
KENT
DA1 2QT
Tel: 01322 407 443

Derbyshire Language Scheme
Market House
Market Place
Ripley
DERBYSHIRE
DE5 3BR
Tel: 01773 748 002

Devon Learning Resources
21 Old Mill Road
Torquay
DEVON
TQ2 6AU,
Tel: 01803 605 531

Down Syndrome Educational Trust (DownsEd)
The Sarah Duffen Centre
Belmont Street
Southsea
HAMPSHIRE
PO5 1NA
Tel: 01705 824 261

Down's Syndrome Association (DSA)
155 Mitcham Road
LONDON
SW17 9PG
Tel: 0181 682 4001

Inclusion Press UK
29 Heron Drive
Poynton
Stockport
CHESHIRE
SK12 1QR
Tel: 01625 859 146

Inclusive Schools Network
University of Cambridge
Institute of Education
Shaftsbury Road
CAMBRIDGE,
CB2 2BX
Tel: 01223 369 631

**Independent Panel for Special
Educational Advice (IPSEA)**
4 Ancient House Mews
Woodbridge
SUFFOLK
IP12 1DH
Tel: 01394 382 814

Learning Development Aids (LDA)
Duke Street
Wisbech
CAMBRIDGESHIRE
PE13 2AE
Tel: 01945 463 441

Network 81
1–7 Woodfield Terrace
Chapel Hill
Stansted
ESSEX
CM24 8AJ
Tel: 01279 647 415

Oxford University Press
Education Division
OXFORD
OX2 6BR
Tel: 01536 741 519

**The Signalong Group Communication
and Language Centre**
All Saints Hospital
Chatham
KENT
ME4 5NG
Tel: 01634 819915

Rickett Educational Media (REM)
Great Western House
Langport
SOMERSET
TA10 9YU
Tel: 01458 253636

St. Joseph's Workshops Ltd.
190/192 Bag Lane
ATHERTON
M46 0JZ
Tel: 01942 883 210

References

Allen, L. (1987) *Like Other Children*. Bristol. Centre for Studies in Inclusive Education.

Alliance for Inclusive Education (1997) *The Green Paper & Inclusive Education*. Consultative document.

Ashman, A., and Elkins, J. (1990) 'Cooperative Learning Among Special Students' in Foot, H., Morgan, M. and Shute, R. *Children Helping Children*. Chichester: John Wiley.

Beadman, J. (1997) *An Evaluation of Educational Placement for Children with Down's Syndrome in the South Devon Education Area*. Devon County Psychological Service.

Bird, G. and Buckley, S. (1994) *Meeting the Educational Needs of Children with Down's Syndrome*. UK: University of Portsmouth.

Booth, T. (1996) 'A Perspective on Inclusion from England', *Cambridge Journal of Education* **26**(1) 87–99

Booth, T., and Potts, P. (1983) *Integrating Special Education*. Oxford: Blackwell.

Bower, A. and Hayes, A. (1994) 'Short-term memory deficits and Down's Syndrome', *Down's Syndrome: Research & Practice* **2**(2), 47–50.

Bray, M. (1995) *Dysfluency, Stammering and Down's Syndrome*. London: British Stammering Association in conjunction with the Down's Syndrome Association.

Broadley, I. (1994) *Teaching Short Term Memory Skills to Children with Down's Syndrome*. Unpublished PhD thesis. UK: University of Portsmouth.

Buckley, S. (1995) 'Teaching reading to teach talking: important new evidence', *Portsmouth Down's Syndrome Trust Newsletter* **5**(5), 1–6.

Buckley, S. and Bird, G. (1993) 'Teaching Children with Down's Syndrome to Read', *Down's Syndrome: Research & Practice* **1**(1), 34–41.

Burns, Y. and Gunn, P. (1993) *Down Syndrome – Moving Through Life*. Chapman & Hall.

Capper, S. (1997) 'Mainstream Schools & the Tribunals', *Down's Syndrome Association Newsletter* **83**, 32.

Cairo, S. (1985) *Our Brother has Down's Syndrome*. Toronto: Annick Press.

Casey, W., Jones, D., Watkins, B. (1988) 'Integration of Down's Syndrome Children in the Primary School', *British Journal of Educational Psychology* **58**, 279–86.

Caswell, J. and Pinner, S. (1996) *SENAT: Special Needs Assistants and Teachers*. Northumberland County Council.

Caycho, L., Gunn, P. and Siegal, M. (1991) 'Counting by children with Down's syndrome', *American Journal of Mental Retardation* **95**(5), 575–83.

Churchill, M. (1993) 'Moving Daniel to Mainstream at 9 Years Old', *Down's Syndrome: Research & Practice* **1**(2), 81–4.

Clayton, T. (1990) 'The Training Needs of Special Welfare Assistants', *Educational & Child Psychology* **7**(1), 44–52.

Comblain, A. (1994) 'Working memory in Down's syndrome: training rehearsal strategy' *Down's Syndrome: Research & Practice* **2**(3), 123–27.

Cooke, N., Heron, T., Heward, W., and Test, D. (1982) 'Integration of a Down's Syndrome Child in a Classwide Peer Tutoring System', *Mental Retardation* **20**, 22–5.

CSIE (1994) *Talking Inclusion*. Bristol: Centre for Studies on Inclusive Education.

CSIE (1996) *Developing an Inclusive Policy for Your School*. Bristol: Centre for Studies on Inclusive Education.

Cuckle, P. (1997) 'School Placement of Pupils with Down's Syndrome in England & Wales', *British Journal of Special Education* **24**(4), 175–80.

Cunningham, C., *et al.* (1998) 'Educational Placements for Children with Down Syndrome', *European Journal of Special Needs Education* **13**(3).

Curry, M. and Bromfield, C. (1994) *Personal and Social Education for Primary Schools through Circle Time*. Stafford: NASEN Publications.

Davies, A. and Richie, D. (1997) *THRASS – Teaching Handwriting, Reading and Spelling Skills*. Glasgow: Collins Educational.

De Wit, T. (ed.) (1994) *All Together (K)now. Possibilities for Integration in Europe, Secondary Education*. Utrecht: Seminarium voor Orthopedagogiek.

DfE (1992) *Getting In on the Act*. London: HMSO.

DfEE (1997a) *Excellence in Schools*. London: HMSO.

DfEE (1997b) *Excellence for All Children: Meeting Special Educational Needs*. London: HMSO.

Dobson, S. (1995) 'How do Speech and Language Therapists Work with Support Assistants Attached to Communication Disabled Children', *Down's Syndrome: Research & Practice*, **3**(1), 19–23.

Dyson, A. and Millward, A. (1997) 'The Transformation of Mainstream Schools' in Pijl, S. Meijer, C., and Hegarty, S. *Inclusive Education: a Global Agenda*. London: Routledge.

Farrell, P. (1997) 'The Integration of Children with Severe Learning Difficulties', *Journal of Applied Research in Intellectual Disabilities* **10**, 1–14.

Faulkener, D. and Lewis, V. (1995) 'Intervention: Down's Syndrome and Autism' in Bancroft, D. and Carr, R. (eds.) *Influencing Children's Development*. Oxford: Blackwell.

Flynn, M. and Flynn, P. (1998) *Thinking About Having a Learning Disability*. London: Belitha Press.

Foot, H., Shute, R., Morgan, M., Barron, A. (1990) 'Theoretical Issues in Peer Tutoring' in Foot, H., Morgan, M., Shute, R. *Children Helping Children*. Chichester: John Wiley.

Gillham, B. (1979) *The First Words Language Programme*. London: Allen & Unwin.

Gillham, B. (1983). *Two Words Together*. London: Allen & Unwin.

Glaesel, B. (1997) 'Integration: A Question of Attitude and Planning' in Pijl, S., Meijer, C., Hegarty, S. *Inclusive Education: a Global Agenda*. London: Routledge.

Graham, G. (1992) *Teaching Children Physical Education: Becoming a Master Teacher*. Illinois. Human Kinetics Books.

Gross, J. (1996) 'Working with Parents', *Special Children* **93**.

Haka-Ikse, K. and Mian, M. (1993) 'Sexuality in Children' *Pediatrics in Review*, **14**(10), 401–7.

Hanrahan, J. and Newman, T. (1996) 'Teaching Addition to Children' in Stratford, R. and Gunn, P. *New Approaches to Down's Syndrome*. London: Cassell.

Hawkridge, D. and Vincent, T. (1992) *Learning Difficulties and Computers*. London: Jessica Kingsley.

Hegarty, S. and Pocklington, K. (1982) *Integration in Action*. Windsor: NFER/Nelson.

Jobling, A. (1994) 'Physical Education for the Person with Down Syndrome: More than Playing Games', *Down's Syndrome: Research & Practice* **2**(1), 31–6.

Kingsley, J. and Levitz, M. (1994) *Count Us In: Growing Up with Down Syndrome*. New York: Harcourt Brace & Co.

Knowles, W. and Masidlover, M. (1982) *The Derbyshire Language Scheme.* Derbyshire County Council.

Kumin, L. (1994) *Communication Skills in Children with Down Syndrome.* Rockville USA: Woodbine House.

Laws, G., MacDonald, J., Buckley, S., Broadley, I. (1995) 'The Influence of Reading Instruction on Language and Memory Development in Children with Down's Syndrome', *Down's Syndrome: Research & Practice* 3(2), 59–65.

Lee, B and Henkhuzens, Z. (1996) *Integration in Progress.* Slough: NFER.

Le Provost, P. (1986) 'The Use of Signing to Encourage First Words' in Buckley, S. et al. *The Development of Language and Reading Skills in Children with Down's Syndrome.* Portsmouth Polytechnic.

Lincoln, J., Batty, J., Townsend, R., Collins, M. (1992) 'Working for Greater Inclusion of Children with Severe Learning Difficulties in Mainstream Secondary Schools', *Educational & Child Psychology* 9(4), 46–51.

Lopez, J. (1994) 'The Integration of Mentally Retarded Children: Analysis of an Experience in Spain', *European Journal of Special Needs Education* 9(2), 145–52.

Lorenz, S. (1984) *Long Term Effects of Early Intervention in Children with Down's Syndrome.* Unpublished PhD thesis, University of Manchester.

Lorenz, S. (1992) 'Supporting Special Needs Assistants in Mainstream Schools', *Educational & Child Psychology* 9(4), 25–33.

Lorenz, S. (1995) 'The Placement of Children with Down's Syndrome: a Survey of One Northern LEA', *British Journal of Special Education* 22(1), 16–20.

Lorenz, S. (1996) *Supporting Support Assistants.* Manchester: Lorenz.

Lorenz, S. (1998) *Effective In-Class Support.* London: David Fulton Publishers.

Lorenz, S, Sloper, P., Cunningham, C., (1985) 'Reading and Down's Syndrome', *British Journal of Special Education* 12(2), 65–70.

MacKenzie, S. and Hulme, C. (1992) *Working Memory and Severe Learning Difficulties.* Hove: Lawrence Erlbaum Associates.

Margerison, A. (1997) 'Class Teachers and the Role of Classroom Assistants in the Delivery of Special Educational Needs', *Support for Learning* 12(4), 166–70.

Mason, M. (1989) *Nothing Special.* London: Working Press.

Mason, M. and Rieser, R. (1994) *Altogether Better.* London: Charity Projects.

Meijer, C., Pijl, S., Hegarty, S. (1994) *New Perspectives in Special Education: a Six-Country Study of Integration.* London: Routledge.

Milicic, N. (1994) *It's Good to be Different.* Bristol: Lucky Duck Publishing.

Moorcroft-Cuckle, P. (1993) 'Type of School Attended by Children with Down's Syndrome', *Educational Research* 35(3), 267–9.

Moyles, J. (1997) *Jills of All Trades? Classroom Assistants in KS1 Classes.* Leicester: University School of Education.

Newbold, D. (1997) '20th Birthday for Integration', *Times Educational Supplement.* 7 November.

Norwich, B. (1997) *A Trend towards Inclusion: Statistics on Special School Placements and Pupils with Statements in Ordinary Schools. England 1992–96.* Bristol: Centre for Studies in Inclusive Education.

O'Brien, J. and Forest, M. (1989) *Action for Inclusion.* Cheshire: Inclusion Press (UK).

Olwein, P. (1995) *Teaching Reading to Children with Down's Syndrome.* USA: Woodbine Press.

O'Grady, R. (1994) 'Cherry at Mainstream Secondary School', *Down's Syndrome: Research & Practice* 2(2), 85–7.

Pearpoint, J. and Forest, M. (1992) *The Inclusion Papers.* Inclusion Press (UK).

Perske, R. (1988) *Circles of Friends.* USA: Abingdon Press.

Petley, K. (1994) 'An Investigation into the Experiences of Parents and Headteachers Involved in the Integration of Primary Aged Children with Down's Syndrome into Mainstream School', *Down's Syndrome: Research & Practice* 2(3), 91–7.

Phillips, D. (1995) 'Accessing the School Community through Student Support Teams'. Poster session presented at ISEC Birmingham.

Philps, C. (1993) *A Comparative Study of the Academic Achievement and Language Development of Children with Down's Syndrome Placed in Mainstream and Special Schools.* Unpublished M.Phil. thesis, University of Wolverhampton.

Pieterse, M. and Treloar, R. (1981) *The Macquarie Program for Developmentally Delayed Children.* Australia: Macquarie University.

Pointer, B. (1993) *Movement Activities for Children with Learning Difficulties.* London: Jessica Kingsley.

Pyke, N. (1997) 'Statistics – and Critics – Aplenty', *Times Educational Supplement,* 21 November. School and College Performance Tables.

Reid, G. and Block, M. (1996) 'Motor Development and Physical Education', in Stratford, B. and Gunn, P. *New Approaches to Down's Syndrome.* London: Cassell.

Rieser, R. and Mason. M. (1992) *Disability Equality in the Classroom.* London: Disability Equality in Education.

Rondal, J. (1996) 'Oral Language in Down's Syndrome' in Rondal *et al., Down's Syndrome: Psychological, Psychobiological and Socio-Educational Perspectives.* London: Whurr Publishers.

Scheepstra, A., Pijl, S., Nakken, H. (1996) 'Knocking on the School Door: Pupils in the Netherlands with Down's Syndrome Enter Regular Education', *British Journal of Special Education* 23(3), 134–9.

Schnorr, P. (1990) 'Part-time Placement for a 7 Year Old with Down Syndrome', *Journal of the Association for Persons with Severe Handicaps* 15, 231–40.

Sebba, J. and Sachdev, D. (1997) *What Works in Inclusive Education?* Ilford. Barnardo's.

Shaw, L. (1997) *Inclusion in Action.* Bristol: Centre for Studies on Inclusive Education.

Shepperdson, B. (1995) 'Changes in School Placements of Pupils with Down Syndrome', *Research in Education* 53, 1–10.

Shotter, D. (1997) 'Smoothing the Way' *Special Children* 103, 22–5.

Sloper, P., Cunningham, C., Turner, S., Knussen, C. (1990) 'Factors Relating to the Academic Attainments of Children with Down's Syndrome', *British Journal of Educational Psychology* 60, 284–98.

Sloper, P. and Turner, S. (1994) *Families of Teenagers with Down Syndrome: Parent, Child and Sibling Adaptation.* University of Manchester: Hester Adrian Research Centre. Final report to ESRC.

Stainback, S., Stainback, W., Stefanich, G., Alper, S. (1996) 'Learning in Inclusive Classrooms' in Stainback, S. and Stainback, W. *Inclusion: a Guide for Educators.* Baltimore: Paul Brookes Publishing.

Tashie, C., *et al.* (1993) *Changes in Latitudes, Changes in Attitudes.* USA: University of New Hampshire.

Testa, M. (1994) *Thumbs Up, Rico.* USA: Albert Whitman.

Thompson, I. (1997) 'Numbers Fall Into Place', *Times Educational Supplement* 3 October, Mathematics Extra.

Thompson, M. (1992) *My Brother, Matthew.* USA: Woodbine House.

UNESCO (1994) *The Salamanca Statement and Framework for Action on Special Needs Education.* Paris: UNESCO.

Vandercook, T., *et al.* (1994) *Lessons for Inclusion.* Minnesota: Inclusion Press.

Van Dyke, D., McBrien, D., Sherbondy, A. (1995) 'Issues of Sexuality in Down Syndrome', *Down's Syndrome: Research & Practice* 3(2), 65–9.

Walker-Hirsch, L. and Champagne, M. (1992) 'Circles III: Safer Ways' in Crocker, H., Cohen, H., Kastner, T. (eds) *HIV Infection and Developmental Disabilities.* Baltimore: Paul H. Brookes.

Warnock, M. (1982) 'Children with Special Needs in Ordinary Schools: Integration Revisited', *Education Today* 32, 56–62.

Watkins, G. and Hunter-Carsch, M. (1995) 'Prompt Spelling: A Practical Approach to Paired Spelling', *Support for Learning* **10**(3), 133–8.

Wertheimer, A. (1997) *Inclusive Education – a Framework for Change*. Bristol: Centre for Studies in Inclusive Education.

Wilson, D. & Newton, C. (1996) 'A Circle of Friends', *Special Children* **89**, 7–9.

Wishart, J. (1993) 'Learning the Hard Way; Avoidance Strategies in Young Children with Down's Syndrome', *Down's Syndrome: Research & Practice* **1**(2), 47–55.

Wishart, J. (1996) 'Learning in Young Children with Down's Syndrome' in Rondal, J. *et al.* (eds) *Down's Syndrome. Psychological, Psychobiological and Socio-Educational Perspectives*. London: Whurr Publishers.

Wolfendale, S. (1997) 'Partnership with Parents: Vision or Reality?' in Wolfendale, S.(ed.) *Partnership with Parents in Action*. Tamworth: NASEN.

Index